THE
PHANTOM
OF THE
CINEMA

*Character in
Modern Film*

L L O Y D
M I C H A E L S

STATE UNIVERSITY OF NEW YORK PRESS

Published by
State University of New York Press, Albany

© 1998 State University of New York

For information, address State University of New York Press,
State University Plaza, Albany, N.Y., 12246

Production by Marilyn P. Semerad
Marketing by Dana E. Yanulavich

Library of Congress Cataloging-in-Publication Data

Michaels, Lloyd.
    The phantom of the cinema : character in modern film / Lloyd
Michaels.
        p.   cm. — (SUNY series, cultural studies in cinema/video)
    Includes bibliographical references and index.
    ISBN 0-7914-3567-9 (hc : alk. paper). — ISBN 0-7914-3568-7 (pb :
alk. paper)
    1. Characters and characteristics in motion pictures. I. Title.
II. Series.
PN1995.9.C36M53 1998
791.43'6—dc21
                                                                97-11383
                                                                    CIP

10 9 8 7 6 5 4 3 2 1

THE
PHANTOM
OF THE
CINEMA

THE SUNY SERIES

CULTURAL STUDIES IN CINEMA/VIDEO

Wheeler Winston Dixon, editor

For Mary

CONTENTS

List of Illustrations   ix

Preface   xiii

Acknowledgments   xix

CHAPTER ONE   1
The Phantom of the Cinema:
Representation of Character in the Modern Film

CHAPTER TWO   33
Reflexivity and Character in *Persona*

CHAPTER THREE   47
Incarnations of the Confidence Man

CHAPTER FOUR   67
Reviving the Undead:
Herzog's Remake of *Nosferatu*

CHAPTER FIVE   83
The Spy and the Cipher

CHAPTER SIX   101
Documenting Character in *The Thin Blue Line*

CHAPTER SEVEN   119
Avatars of Memory:
Entropy and Nostalgia in the Representation of Character

CHAPTER EIGHT   139
Conclusion:
The Mystery and Melancholy of a Self

Notes   165

Works Cited and Consulted   173

About the Author   181

Index   183

LIST OF ILLUSTRATIONS

FIGURE 1. *Jules and Jim*. Courtesy Jerry Ohlinger's   14

FIGURE 2. *Escape from Alcatraz*   19

FIGURE 3. *The Day of the Jackal*   21

FIGURE 4. *The Day of the Jackal*   21

FIGURE 5. *The Day of the Jackal*   22

FIGURE 6. *The Day of the Jackal*   23

FIGURE 7. *Reservoir Dogs*   27

FIGURE 8. *Persona*. Courtesy Museum of Modern Art   38

FIGURE 9. *Persona*. Courtesy Museum of Modern Art   40

FIGURE 10. *Persona*   42

FIGURE 11. *The Magician*   56

FIGURE 12. *House of Games*   63

FIGURE 13. *House of Games*   65

FIGURE 14. *Nosferatu, a Symphony of Horror.* Courtesy Museum of Modern Art   73

FIGURE 15. *Nosferatu, the Vampyre*   79

FIGURE 16. *Nosferatu, the Vampyre.* Courtesy Museum of Modern Art   80

FIGURE 17. *Nosferatu, the Vampyre*   81

FIGURE 18. *Reilly: Ace of Spies.* Courtesy Thames Television   93

FIGURE 19. *The Mystery of Kaspar Hauser*   98

FIGURE 20. *The Thin Blue Line*   112

FIGURE 21. *The Thin Blue Line*   113

FIGURE 22. *The Thin Blue Line*   115

FIGURE 23. *The Thin Blue Line*   116

FIGURE 24. *Lacombe, Lucien.* Courtesy Museum of Modern Art   132

FIGURE 25. *Lacombe, Lucien.* Courtesy Jerry Ohlinger's   135

FIGURE 26. *Daddy Nostalgia*   137

FIGURE 27. *Mephisto*   141

FIGURE 28. *Badlands*   145

FIGURE 29. *Days of Heaven.* Courtesy Museum of Modern Art   149

FIGURE 30. *Days of Heaven*   151

FIGURE 31. *Five Easy Pieces*   154

FIGURE 32. *Five Easy Pieces*   155

FIGURE 33. *The Lacemaker*   158

FIGURE 34. *The Lacemaker*   159

PREFACE

─────────────── ◈ ───────────────

While editing the journal *Film Criticism* for the past twenty years and conducting research in preparation for writing this book, I have been surprised to discover how little attention has been paid to either a general theory of fictional character or the construction of character within specific texts. Writing about literature, W. J. Harvey observed this dearth of interest in his *Character in the Novel* (1965): "Modern criticism, by and large, has relegated the treatment of character to the periphery of its attention . . . and has regarded it more often as a misguided and misleading abstraction" (192). A decade later, Seymour Chatman remarked upon the same phenomenon in *Story and Discourse: Narrative Structure in Fiction and Film* (1978): "It is remarkable how little has been said about the theory of character in literary history and criticism" (107). In *Life Made Real: Characterization in the Novel since Proust and Joyce* (1991), Thomas Petruso further describes how "from the New Critics' injunction against biographical and intentional considerations to the poststructuralists' preoccupation with textual antics, characterization—and particularly its relation to real-life models—has been either ignored or relegated to the category of literary gossip or anecdote" (1). And most recently, Murray Smith notes in *Engaging Characters: Fiction, Emotion, and the Cinema* (1995) that his own argument for the "saliency" of characters in the study of film narrative remains "deeply unfashionable" (4).

This resistance to theorizing character probably results from the extensive influence of the structuralist and poststructuralist attacks on representation throughout the period. Adopting descriptions of characters as little more than "semic codes" (Roland Barthes), "actantial structures" (Umberto Eco), or "sets of predicates grouped under proper names" (Jonathan Culler), formalist arguments have generally criticized the "thematizing" of character as reductive, conservative, and even (in the eyes of Hélène Cixous and her followers) oppressive. While this view has undoubtedly held sway over a generation of narrative theorists, in its preoccupation with textuality it has often misconstrued the creative process and ignored the material evidence of reception. Yet despite such indifference and condemnation, the concept of character, it seems obvious, has never been seriously threatened for either filmmakers or spectators, no matter how ideologically complicit or naive they may have been branded.

Because its signifying process is rooted in photography, the cinema has been, from its inception, associated with representation by both documentarists and fiction filmmakers. But representation, properly conceived, involves not simply the mirroring of external reality—that *would* be a reductive, oppressive theory—but the creation of a world, in Brian Rosenberg's phrase, that "recalls, partially resembles, and otherwise relates to a prior one" (12). From this view, a character may be simply but adequately defined as a "represented person" (Phelan 27). As such, characters have continued to claim the attention of professional screenwriters, who customarily focus their scripts around them, reviewers, who regularly evaluate their credibility, morality, and capacity to inspire speculation, and ordinary audiences, who stubbornly cling to characters as objects for contemplation reaching well beyond the limits of the language or narrative structure supposedly confining them.

While insisting on the representational aspect of film characters as the rationale for a neo-mimetic approach to understanding their potential resonance—a premise rooted in the fact that the cinematic signifier (a photographic image projected at twenty-four frames per second) is less abstract, more closely related to its signified (whether understood as an historical personage, an actor, or a fictional character) than the printed word—my study also acknowledges the fact that characters in the cinema, unlike those on the theatrical stage, are, quite literally, *flat*, to borrow E. M. Forster's famous term, as well as larger than life—at least before the advent of television and video transmission. They were once *really there*, but are now really absent except for their exhibition as *recordings*. This synthetic aspect of filmic representation, of course, has formed the basis of the structuralist critique of character. Rather than decisively underscoring the constructed quality of film characters, however, such slipperiness may paradoxically reinforce their mimetic function. James Phelan has touched on this point by questioning the assumption that we know what a person is when we encounter one in life. Real persons, experience seems to tell us, are frequently easy to meet but very difficult to understand. It is this evanescence and mystery of character as found in the movies and in life that interests me here.

The Phantom of the Cinema examines the ways in which a particular kind of movie (most, but not all, being associated with the art cinema; most, but not all, being identified as modernist or postmodernist texts) deconstructs the notion of character as stable, knowable, and nameable while still retaining a claim on the figure's representativeness. Beginning with the concept of "presence of absence" frequently invoked to distinguish cinema from other performative arts by a broad spectrum of theorists including André Bazin, Christian Metz, and Stanley Cavell, I will argue for film-in-general's propensity to present images that reflect this century's consciousness of a constantly mediated reality and of a problematic human identity. At the risk of espousing the twin heresies of aestheticism and essentialism, I proceed from the same belief as Cavell that "pride of place within the canon of serious films will be found occupied by those films that most clearly and most deeply discover the powers of the medium itself, those that give fullest significance to the possibilities and necessities of its physical basis" (219). I then attempt to explain how various individual films explore the complex, ambiguous, and elusive nature of character. These "phantoms of the cinema," I argue, continue to haunt our imagination and memory because, as mimetic representations, they reflect our unrequited desire for human contact, and because, as formal elements in cinematic narrative, they remind us of the camera's capacity to deceive as well as to reveal. In either case, these spectral figures compel our attention by their very quality of remaining unpossessible.

When I began this analysis of the ambiguous and reflexive incarnations of film character, my resistance to the structuralist critique and the cognitive models that have recently taken over film studies struck me as either retrograde ("idealist" or "ahistorical," some might say) or on the cutting edge. As the project developed, however, new books in literary and film studies by the aforementioned scholars and others encouraged my line of thought at the risk of making the completed argument seem almost mainstream. If I can now stake any claims to originality for The Phantom of the Cinema, they may rest with my consistent emphasis on character, the element among the triadic signifieds of narrative (the others being events and setting) least widely discussed, and in my attempt to connect a particular kind of character with cinematic self-reflexivity.

Neither a totalizing theory of film character nor a comprehensive taxonomy of character types, my study eschews any such *grand syntagmatique* in favor of an effort to account for the powerful effect of certain fugitive, spectral protagonists within a narrow but persistent range of cinematic narratives. To borrow a phrase from Truffaut (and Robert Ray), I am attempting to trace a certain tendency within the modern cinema. In this enterprise, I have exposed myself as both an inveterate interpreter and an unabashed "art film guy." I suppose I stand halfway between postmodernist theory's "critique of the hermeneutic" (Jameson 12) and a more traditional humanistic approach: that is, I employ interpretive strategies to illustrate the text's own critique of the efficacy of interpreting character. Although my work rests on several foundational theories put forth by Christian Metz (lost object status of film), Robert Stam (self-reflexivity), John Ellis (historicity of the image), and others, I ultimately seek to subordinate the seductiveness of theory to the entrancement of the true object of my study, selected texts of the modern cinema. The idea for the book originated with my noticing a common thread—conceptualized as "the phantom of character"—running through a series of independent essays composed over a number of years. While I readily draw upon several theoretical models to help explain certain unconscious processes during viewing, I remain committed to the task of criticism, which is to propose refined ways of understanding how specific texts instigate those processes. The methodology that informed these essays and is elaborated in this book thus seeks both to explain the intricate strategies of certain compelling films and to define their special significance among mainstream movies and the art cinema.

In straying from the parameters of a structuralist approach, I have sought to restore a balance that fully acknowledges the role of author and spectator as well as the text itself in the experience of responding to what I would call "serious" films. This project involves reconciling the humanist account of character as the representation of an autonomous self with the structuralist emphasis on textuality, a process that has led me to an understanding of character not as an *empty* signifier but as a *fleeting* one. All of the works that engage me here create a tension between narrational devices that clarify the spectator's comprehension of character by conforming with institutional practices and those that complicate it by subverting or disturbing those accepted norms. Through my analysis of the affinity between the cinema's signifying system, which employs a ghostly image of an absent referent, and the construction of these "phantoms of the cinema," I hope to illuminate some sound reasons for granting a privileged place to those films that project most clearly the haunting character of the medium itself.

ACKNOWLEDGMENTS

◈

The work that eventually became this book began at the 1977 National Endowment for the Humanities Summer Seminar in film theory at the University of Iowa under the direction of Dudley Andrew. I am grateful to the NEH for its initial support and to Dudley for his enduring encouragement and friendship. My return to Iowa City in the summer of 1995 was funded by a faculty development grant from Allegheny College. During the period when the project took shape and was written, I was fortunate to have release time through the help of the college. Special thanks to President Dan Sullivan, who appointed me to the Frederick F. Seely professorship, and to Dean Jim Bulman, who nominated me for the Seely chair and whose warm friendship over twenty years has contributed so much to my affection for this place. I also have benefited from the collegiality of friends in the English Department—Jeanne Braham, Diane D'Amico, Diane Goodman, Sonya Jones, David Miller, Laura Quinn, Ben Slote, Paul Zolbrod, and especially Brian Rosenberg, who has offered a model of lucid scholarship in his own writing on character and who generously shared portions of his research at a crucial stage in the development of my manuscript.

Earlier versions of portions of this book have previously appeared in *Literature/Film Quarterly*, *New Orleans Review*, *Post Script*, *University of Toronto Quarterly*, and *Film Criticism*. Thanks to the editors of these journals for permission to use this material. Dorothy Smith was extremely helpful in proofreading the galleys and preparing the index. I am also grateful for the steadfast support of Wheeler Winston Dixon, Clay Morgan, Marilyn Semerad, and the readers and editors at State University of New York Press.

Back at Iowa in 1977 I met a fellow participant who was to become my closest friend and colleague in the field of film studies. Arthur Nolletti has been a constant source of knowledge, inspiration, and good fellowship (albeit nearly always over the phone) throughout my editorship of *Film Criticism* and work on this book. Indeed, he has been my "ideal reader" as *The Phantom of the Cinema* was being written and a most diligent actual reader once the manuscript was completed. His praise has been almost as welcome as his gentle but firm criticism; I am lucky to have him as my own phantom *cineaste* in the production of this work.

Finally, a word of thanks to my son Jack, not only for the use of his computer but for all those wonderful moments of watching sports together when I could put aside the pursuit of the cinema's slippery characters for the pleasure of real companionship. And heartfelt gratitude to my wife, Mary, the most important "character" in my life and the best movie date a guy could desire: every page bears the trace of her inspiring presence. The curiosity, discipline, and love of beautiful images that inform her work have been the touchstones of my own approach to understanding film art.

CHAPTER ONE

◈

The Phantom of the Cinema: Representation of Character in the Modern Film

DERSHOWITZ: "You're a very strange man."
VON BULOW: "You have no idea."

—*Reversal of Fortune*

"CLOSER TO LIFE"

The history of literary criticism in the western world may be said to have originated in an ongoing debate over the value of representation, between Plato's mistrust of mimesis as intrinsically deceptive, emotionally disturbing, and morally misleading and Aristotle's description of the same process as serious, orderly, and cathartic. In our own times, the most influential theorists—followers of Brecht, the New Critics, and Barthes, for example—have extended the Platonic attack on representation, repeatedly questioning the merits of the reader's identification with characters as if they were real and not textual effects of the plot. Critics who have persisted in treating fictional characters as representative persons have often been rather summarily consigned to a category formerly reserved for Shakespeare's groundlings and the popcorn-chewing habitués of drive-in movies: members of a *naive* audience.

1

Viewed historically, the successive attempts of Russian formalists, New Critics, structuralists, and poststructuralists to objectify the study of narrative by excluding the intentionality and personality of authors on the one hand and the emotional and imaginative responses of readers on the other seems to parallel a development in post-Romantic art towards the creation of authorless texts. There is hardly space here to survey the case against characters; readers of this book will no doubt be familiar with its outlines. Briefly stated, the argument emphasizes the synthetic aspect of all narrative, thus the inevitable artificiality of characters. From different perspectives, Brecht and Barthes (one might as readily have cited Propp and Culler—the list of prominent narratologists who denigrate characterization is hardly limited) have described characters as products of the plot, serving as its agents. "Character is a construction of the text," film theorist Edward Branigan has summarized the structuralist position, "not *a priori* and autonomous" (12). Rather than being analogous to real persons, characters are best understood as *conventions*, narrative elements attached to proper names and more like metaphors or chapter titles than people we might meet in everyday life.

At first glance, the cinema would appear to be less vulnerable than literary fiction to the structuralist/semiotics critique of representation—though perhaps more susceptible to the Brechtian/ideological analysis—if only because its sign is more closely related to its referent. Beginning with the introduction of photography, the automatic aspect of the production of images satisfied a long-held wish of representational art to "escape subjectivity" (Cavell 21). According to Jean-Louis Baudry, the invention of the cinematic apparatus fulfilled a dream "to construct a simulation machine capable of offering the subject perceptions which are really representations mistaken for perceptions" (705). Recent scholars like Gregory Currie, however, have challenged Baudry's premise for the "ideological effects" of the apparatus, re-opening the possibilities for a neo-mimetic theoretical approach by arguing against the notion that film "is typically productive of any cognitive illusion to the effect that what it represents is real; our standard mode of engagement with the film is via imagination rather than belief . . . But while the pictures of film are not productive of illusions, they are typically realistic pictures: pictures which are like, in significant ways, the things they represent" (280). Murray Smith has sensibly summarized this critique of Baudry's reception theory: "Indeed, praising something for its 'realism' depends implicitly on recognizing that it is not of the same order as the thing imitated, that an effort of construction was necessary to produce the effect. In other words, that it is conventional" (*Characters* 33). Aside from the fact that no serious critic has ever argued that film characters are real, it seems at least reasonable to consider a movie character as a "possible person"—the view that will be taken here—when she is represented by a real person, or, more properly, the image of a real person formed by light reflecting off a real performer and reacting with a chemical emulsion. While the novel *strains*, in other words, to represent an action, setting, or character, the fiction film seems to come by such mimetic effects quite naturally. In fact, the very autonomous quality of the cinematic image may account for the relatively slow advance of a sophisticated film theory, as Christian Metz has suggested, since movies are usually difficult to talk about because they are easy to understand.

Pressed first by the invention of photography and soon after by motion pictures, modern novelists have been forced to confront the limitations of language in depicting external reality. In part as a result of cinema's ascendancy, the development of the novel in the twentieth century may be described as having shifted its concern away from complex plots towards in-depth characterization (Petruso 10). Joseph Conrad, writing at the very moment of film's emergence as a means of popular storytelling, defined his task as an author in visual terms: "to make you *see*" (147), the same terms D. W. Griffith would later use to describe the filmmaker's art. The immediate impact of motion pictures was not lost on an author as rooted in nineteenth-century novelistic traditions as Leo Tolstoy, who, on his eightieth birthday in 1908, recognized the radical transformation the new medium would bring to narrative literature and yet celebrated its apparent fulfillment of the writer's grandest aspiration:

> You will see that the little clicking contraption with the revolving handle will make a revolution in our life—in the life of writers. It is a direct attack on the old methods of literary art. We shall have to adapt ourselves to the shadowy screen and to the cold machine. A new form of writing will be necessary. I have thought of that and I can feel what is coming.
>
> But I rather like it. The swift change of scene, this blending of emotion and experience—it is much better than the heavy, long-drawn-out kind of writing to which we are accustomed. It is closer to life. In life, too, changes and transitions

flash by before our eyes, and emotions of the soul are like a hurricane. The cinema has divined the mystery of motion. And that is its greatness. (Starr 32)

In describing the ascendancy of motion pictures as the new century's preeminent narrative form, Tolstoy struck a balance between the cinema's unique representational aspect (bringing its images "closer to life") and its equally significant capacity for rendering those images as "shadowy," fleeting, and disruptive. This evanescence he also equates with being closer to life.

The cinematic signifier is neither a pure construction (a conception formed in the mind of a reader) nor an unmediated perception; thus, the reality/convention dichotomy that has been posed between theorizing characters as autonomous persons or as textual functions serves little purpose beyond setting up a straw man argument against misguided humanist critics who stand accused of confusing representations for independent agents. Baruch Hochman has proposed a modified mimetic approach to character that opposes Branigan's premise but resists the problem of reification, one that applies even more forcefully to our experience of watching films than of reading novels: "[T]here is a profound congruity between the ways in which we apprehend characters in literature, documented figures in history, and people of whom we have what we think of as direct knowledge in life" (36). The comprehension of characters in literature and film ultimately involves both textual construction and readerly reconstruction.

No definitive theory or taxonomy of character will be attempted in this study. Nearly all such efforts to date conclude, as does John Frow, that character remains "the most problematic and the most undertheorized of the basic categories of narrative theory" (227), a term that "cannot be reduced to exact rules or to a comprehensive statement" (229). At the same time, Rawdon Wilson decides that, in spite of its elusiveness, character is "a concept . . . that the study of literature cannot do without" (749). In light of such of such disclaimers, I am tempted to begin this study as one of my celebrated graduate school professors used to begin his lectures: by saying, "I mean by the term 'myth' what everyone else means," and be done with the problem. Instead, I will define character as *a represented person that corresponds by analogy to our understanding of personhood in real life without being confused with reality*, a term too often conflated with verisimilitude.

In most fictional narratives, as structuralists have correctly pointed out, characters, "as opposed to people in life, intrinsically mean something" (Hochman 66), wherein we may discover the most profound dissimilarity between the two realms of art and reality. Because characters consist of a more or less selective "paradigm of traits" (Chatman, Story 126) representing an abiding personality (at least before the advent of poststructuralism's attack on the very concept of unified personhood), they inevitably take on a thematic aspect that threatens to obscure their synthetic (formal) status at the same time it promises to enhance our pleasure in and comprehension of the text. The characters that interest me here are not those whose traits readily resolve themselves into a recognizable type—the rogue cop Dirty Harry, the amorous double agent James Bond, the blessed innocent Forrest Gump, even the complex gangster Vito Corleone—but those whose resistance to meaning becomes the dominant paradigm of their characterization. I am interested in them for two reasons: first, because they correspond more closely than the majority of representative types to my own experience encountering historical figures and personal acquaintances in real life, and secondly, because they seem to express a fundamental truth about my experience of encountering them in the movie theater.

THE PRESENCE OF ABSENCE

While the signifier in the cinema may be, as Tolstoy noted, "closer to life" than language (upon which modern film narrative also depends) and thus perhaps better suited to convey the sensation of witnessing physical reality, early movie makers—following the example of primitive photographers[1]—were quick to display the medium's capacity to manipulate, distort, and transform the material presences it recorded. Georges Méliès became the first exhibitor to exploit his audience's acceptance of the projected image as an accurate, reliable tracing of objects and events actually present before the camera. (The Lumières presumably did not calculate the frightened response to their film of a train entering the station.) When Méliès first made a person suddenly disappear in The Vanishing Lady (1896) and replaced her with a skeleton (Fischer 339), he discovered "the conjurer's art" that Ingmar Bergman has equated with the activity of filmmaking itself:

And even today I remind myself with childish excitement that I am really a conjurer, since cinematography is based on deception of the human eye. . . . I perform conjuring tricks with apparatus so expensive and so wonderful that any entertainer in history would have given anything to have it. (Four Screenplays 15)

Méliès's demonstration that the camera *could* lie, that it could transform an omnibus into a hearse or a woman into a cadaverous double, significantly expanded the horizons of both film production and reception. By introducing a remarkable toolbox of special effects (including slow motion, fast motion, reverse motion, freeze frame, double exposure, and process shots), Méliès became the first of many artists of the silent cinema to deconstruct what André Bazin called the audience's "faith in the image" (1:24) as an unmediated recording of reality. In addition to photography's affinity for transcribing material presence, the cinema had illustrated the potential to project an *absence* of the natural order.

Film theorists at least as far back as Arnheim have emphasized this dialectical tension in the movies. "Cinema as a photographic medium instantly poses its images and sounds as recorded phenomena, whose construction occurred in another time and another place. Yet though the figures, objects and places represented are absent from the space in which the viewing takes place, they are also (and astoundingly) present" (Ellis 38). At the same time Méliès was re-creating the effects of a seance in *L'Armoire des frères Davenport* (1902), Edwin S. Porter, a director firmly identified with the realist tradition, created a somewhat less deliberate image of the new medium's capacity to project the uncanny. The famous close-up of the outlaw shooting directly at the camera in *The Great Train Robbery* (1903) has remained so strangely compelling because it portrays in blatant terms the medium's play of presence and absence. Porter's cowboy thus becomes the first phantom of the cinema. His appearance lies outside the parameters of the narrative; indeed, he might be seen either at the very beginning or the very end of the film, depending on the exhibitor's preference. In any case, he receives no special attention within the diegesis. Through his dead-pan expression as he looks directly at the camera and fires his revolver, he both acknowledges our presence and disavows it. "The depth of the automatism of photography is to be read not alone in its mechanical production of an image of reality," Cavell has observed, "but in its mechanical defeat of our presence to that reality. The audience in a theater can be defined as those to whom the actors are present while they are not present to the actors" (25). For Porter's original audience, this absence might be measured by the ineffectuality of the shooting gun as well as by the ambiguity of the actor's expression; for us, it is compounded by the antiquity of the image, most evident in the absence of sound. The reflexivity of this phantom character, of course, is conveyed not only by the visual pun on "shooting" but by his acknowledgment of the camera maintaining the presentness of his world by virtue of our absence.

The concept of presence of absence became central to psychoanalytic film theory after its elaboration in Christian Metz's landmark essay, "The Imaginary Signifier," which has deeply influenced my own speculations about film character. His formulation of the ontology of the cinematic image remains neither wholly original (Arnheim and Bazin having made similar observations without the psychoanalytic framework) nor definitive, but it does offer a way of synthesizing the issues of representation and identification that have proven so problematic in theoretical discussions of character.

> The unique position of the cinema lies in this dual character of its signifier: unaccustomed perceptual wealth, but at the same time stamped with unreality to an unusual degree, and from the very outset. More than the other arts, or in a more unique way, the cinema involves us in the imaginary.(45)

Against the "unaccustomed perceptual wealth" of the magnified image of a cowboy firing his gun directly at the camera, one might say, there is the "unreality" of the action's total lack of consequence, given our "irreducible distance" (Ellis 58) from it. This stamp of unreality ("Every film is a fiction film," Metz argues [44]) follows from the fundamental conditions of film production and reception: the fact that during *shooting*, the actor is present before the camera when the spectator is absent, while during *projection*, only the spectator is present before the screen when the actor is absent. Ellis has described this separation in temporal as well as spatial terms, stressing the inherent historicity in film's signifying process: "The cinema image is marked by a particular half-magic feat in that it makes present something that is absent. The movement shown on the screen is passed and gone when it is called back into being as illusion" (58).

The cinema's mode of signification can be distinguished from those of the novel and the play precisely through this imaginary aspect of the film image. What is projected on the screen involves both *presentation* (unaccustomed perceptual wealth as in the size, luminosity, and detail of the photographic image[2]) and *withdrawal* (not simply the spectator's distance from the screen but her normally repressed knowledge of the image's unreality). Everything perceived in the movies—landscape, decor, objects, and, it will be soon argued, particularly human figures—is, in effect, a scene screened.

Noël Carroll has forcefully questioned the significance of presence/absence as an essential quality of film by arguing that neither Metz nor Ellis takes into account the fictional nature of theater, from which cinema has supposedly been distinguished. "Once we are considering the realm of fiction," Carroll writes, "it makes no sense to speak of the differences between cinema and theater in terms of what is absent to the spectator. In both fictional film and theatrical fiction, the characters are absent from the continuum of our world in the same way." Therefore, he concludes, "Shylock is no more present to the theater spectator than Fred C. Dobbs is present to the film viewer" (38). But Carroll's point holds true only for the referent (the reader's or viewer's mental construct of a particular character) rather than the signifier (the actor). The fact remains that Olivier is actually present on stage in the role of Shylock, while Bogart is not in the movie theater. "The issue of presence of absence which Metz raises has no relevance," Carroll concludes, "where what is being communicated is first and foremost fictional" (38–39). But the issue here concerns not *what* the cinema signifies, but *how* and *to what effect*. By creating a kind of nostalgia for the evanescent image at the very moment of its luminous projection, the cinema replenishes the spectator's desire to see and to know precisely what remains irreparably removed from sight.

This nostalgia for the absent object applies to thematized places (Monument Valley and the national myth of freedom) and things ("Rosebud" and the personal myth of childhood innocence), but resonates most profoundly, I would argue, when attached to characters, who remain in real life both partially hidden (character in the sense of a matrix of emotional, moral, and cognitive traits too complex ever to be entirely comprehended) and subject to change. Unlike Xanadu, the "character" that Thompson searches for in *Citizen Kane* (1941), as the newsreel ironically confirms, cannot be photographed, and who this character apparently once was in Colorado and in the *Inquirer* office, he is no longer in Xanadu. As the modern novel in the hands of Joyce, Proust, and Faulkner turned inward to depict the psychological dimensions of character less accessible to the camera, the cinema generally sought to compensate for its alleged deficiency in representing consciousness through a variety of theatrical strategies.

CHARACTER PRESENTED

When D. W. Griffith defined the filmmaker's task in the same terms—"to make you *see*"—as Conrad had used in reference to the novelist's craft a decade earlier, he referred not to the literal act of perception whereby audiences recognized images projected on a screen as equivalent to observable objects in the real world, but to the interpretive process by which those images acquired certain moral, historical, dramatic, poetic, and psychological meanings that gave off an aura of truth. The camera had allowed us to see; the filmmaker held the power to make us believe. Most narrative films, including those of Méliès, have therefore foregrounded spectacle and continuity in order to stabilize (or "suture," in Oudart's term) the spectator's acceptance of the representational element of the images. Mainstream cinema has relied on at least five institutionalized practices through which character is conventionally constructed, that is, *given*, made present in fullness and comprehensible in relation to norms of reality and the surface of life. Generally associated with drama on the stage, these strategies for presenting character—specifying motives, clarifying nuances, effacing inconsistencies, revealing secret desires—can be categorized as follows: (1) dialogue, (2) the star system, (3) typology, (4) performance style, (5) mise-en-scène.

Characters in movies and plays are perhaps most obviously defined by what they say and what others say about them. To choose an exemplary screenplay centrally concerned with the problem of personal identity, the text of *Citizen Kane* (doubtlessly influenced by Conrad's *Heart of Darkness* as much as by Welles's own theatrical experience) offers five successive narrative perspectives that certainly accumulate rich information about the protagonist. It is not, however, a comprehensive understanding, else the reporter Thompson's ultimate disclaimer ("I don't think any word can explain a man's life") would not be necessary. Sometimes a particularly memorable or witty line can encapsulate two or more characters at once, as in Maddie's seductive observation about Ned in *Body Heat* (1981): "You're not very smart. I like that in a man."

The presence of Kathleen Turner and William Hurt in this popular movie illustrates a second familiar means—the star system—by which films in the tradition of classical Hollywood cinema define character. Audiences identify certain traits of personality, morality, and behavior with the recurrent roles portrayed by certain well-known actors. The thematic associations of Bogart (then) and Eastwood (now) supersede the proper names Sam Spade or Harry Callahan as indicators of character within the particular movies in which these actors appear. This institutional practice is, of course, an immensely rich area for theoretical discussion and debate, but my concern here is merely to repeat the commonplace that type casting has become an established technique for filling in the gaps of a script and constructing a recognizable person.[3] The star persona has proven to be an efficient vehicle for quickly delineating character and allowing the spectator to focus on setting and plot.

Following the long-established model of theatrical characterization, the cinema has employed a nearly infinite array of stereotypes enabling audiences to apprehend quickly and confidently the representative role of a given figure. Baruch Hochman has implicitly defended this narrative device by noting how "our perception of people is typological, in life as well as in literature" (46). Against the structuralist and ideological critiques of this kind of characterization, James Phelan reminds us that, "Although people may have representative significance, they typically cannot be adequately summed up by their representativeness. And the same goes for [fictional] characters" (27). Examples of filmic typology need hardly be listed here, as the topic has preoccupied countless cultural and genre studies, except to note that "character" itself has become a definable type, an identity locked into its own persistent eccentricities, as in Robin Williams's roles in *Good Morning Vietnam* (1987), *The Dead Poet's Society* (1989), and *The Fisher King* (1991).

Williams's highly theatrical performance style illustrates the fourth way in which films traditionally present a comprehensible character. Through such signifiers as facial expression, gesture, and voice, actors on stage and screen offer data suggesting implicit or hidden truths about their character's personal history, motivation, or imperfectly repressed impulses, as when Brando tries on Eva Marie Saint's white glove in *On the Waterfront* (1954) or Streep inflects a Polish accent in *Sophie's Choice* (1982).

Finally, as in a novel or play, film characters become defined by their milieu: the physical surroundings, clothing, and possessions that contribute to our comprehension of who they are. Bazin celebrated the cinema's capacity for rendering different spatial areas with equal clarity through the shot-in-depth as the medium's unique means of presenting characters in relation to their environment. Framing, masking, camera angles, and montage can also serve to clarify a character's identity, as in the low-angle views of Hitler against the background of a brilliant sky in *Triumph of the Will* (1935), transforming an historical figure into a mythic one. Sherlock Holmes's rooms at 221B Baker Street, his deerstalker and meerschaum pipe, his hypodermic needle and seven-percent solution may better serve to illustrate the simple point about mise-en-scène since they reappear so prominently as signifiers of the fictional detective in stage and screen adaptations of Doyle's stories. Such details—the sled and the glass ball in *Citizen Kane* may be the most famous—function to objectify character and then to give it resonance.

CINEMATIC LOSS AND THE
WITHDRAWAL OF CHARACTER

By such commonly recognized techniques as dialogue, casting, generic conventions, acting, costuming, and mise-en-scène are characters *presented* in the cinema. But how can they be, in less obvious ways, simultaneously *withdrawn*, leaving us to contemplate (at least to sense) the "certain but fugitive testimony" (Barthes, Camera 93) that has brought them into being? Drawing on Lacanian psychoanalysis (the mirror stage), Metz has posited that this withdrawal is both inevitable and vital to the cinema's appeal to the imaginary. The specific mode of cinematic signification projects a "lost object" that becomes desirable precisely because it is given only "in effigy, inaccessible from the outset, in a primordial *elsewhere*" (Imaginary 61). As in other forms of voyeurism, the film spectator's pleasure derives from the survival of the gap that separates her from this unpossessible image.

Our comprehension of character on the screen thus simultaneously involves a transcendence of film's imaginary signifier when we come to recognize, understand, or identify with the fictional figure as well as an implicit acknowledgment of the imaginary when that same comprehension becomes clouded, contradictory, or entirely lost. As a result of the cinema's "pure contingency . . . it is always *something* that is represented)" (Barthes, Camera 28), our awareness that the camera does not lie about the fact of the actor (or body double) having once actually appeared before it, we experience that same sense of contact we feel in watching a play—or in meeting a person face-to-face; but because we also know that the film actor impersonating a fictional character is not really there on the screen, we must imagine the presence of what has only been represented in shadow and light, as we would to a much greater degree in reading a novel, where there is not even a tracing except in the mind's eye—or in recalling a person we have not seen in some time. The mirror that the cinema holds up to nature leaves us, like Melville's Ishmael gazing at the "tormenting, mild image" reflected off the water in the first chapter of *Moby Dick*, to contemplate "the ungraspable phantom of life."

Metz's discussion of the *lack* that is the source of replenished desire in the cinema needs to be broadened to encompass several other senses in which film conveys a more diffusive sense of loss. In addition to the spatial separation inscribed both by the spectator's distance from the screen and, more decisively, by the original object's retreat to "a primordial *elsewhere*," the signifying system of film involves the passing of *time* and *energy*. The first of these elements, of course, has long been noted in contrasting film from theater. Susan Sontag, for example, anticipates Ellis's emphasis by noting the inherent historicity of the cinema:

> This youngest of the arts is also the most heavily burdened with memory. . . . Movies preserve the past, theatres—no matter how devoted to the classics, to old plays—can only "modernize." . . . The historical flavor of anything registered on celluloid is so vivid that practically all films older than two years or so are saturated with a kind of pathos. . . . Films age (being objects) as no theatre-event does (being always new). (Film 260)

This recognition that the projected world no longer exists by virtue of its status as a recording contradicts, or at least complicates, the "commonplace" perpetuated by Chatman that "cinema can occur only in the present time" (Story 84).

Like the debate over the status of characters, the discussion of "tense" in the cinema remains long-standing and unresolved. In most instances, the film viewer suspends disbelief in the present-

ness (as well as presence) of the image by ignoring the fact of its production at an earlier time. This psychic process especially applies
to watching a film in its initial theatrical release (aided by the institution's typical strategy of avoiding specifically dated images or references), although frequently enough filmmakers deliberately
evoke an awareness of the medium's ontological pastness, as when
Bogdanovich shoots *The Last Picture Show* (1971) in black-and-
white or when Jeanne Moreau appears as a fictional actress of faded
beauty in *The Last Tycoon* (1976) and *La femme Nikita* (1990).The
spectator's comprehension of Moreau's character within these
films is deeply informed by recalling her younger roles during the
French New Wave. Of course, this kind of nostalgia commonly
affects any retrospective viewing of classical Hollywood movies (in
which we view the ghostly representatives of not only fictional
characters but of celebrated performers nearly all of whom are now
dead) as well as canonical works like *Citizen Kane*, where we may
be struck by Welles's ironic anticipation of his own career, or Truffaut's *Jules and Jim* (1961), where the long-held close-up of
Moreau's still-beautiful reflection in the dressing mirror as she
creams her face reveals the first signs of Catherine's aging, rhymes
with the earlier slide image of the island statue's eroding features,
and foreshadows the inevitable decay of Moreau's own screen
allure (fig. 1). Similarly, if more mundanely, even contemporary
commercial releases and home movies are marked by history:
Demi Moore's old haircut, last summer's bathing suit. Thus, films
remain time-bound in certain ways that novels and staged works
generally are not.[4] The practice of colorizing "old" movies (some
made less than forty years ago) has not succeeded in bringing the
images up-to-date; ironically, the pallid, uniform new colors merely
make the figures seem more ghostly. Film characters may be resur-
rected during projection but only as spectres from the recorded past,
not really there in present time as well as space. To the concept of
presence of absence must be added the presence of pastness, medi-
ating the immediacy and definition of the perceptual experience.

The third way in which the cinematic signifier inscribes a
sense of loss has been less widely discussed than the spatial and
temporal aspects. Quite literally, movies *unwind* through the projector, a process of self-depletion that inexorably (at least prior to
the widespread home use of video playback) results in an empty
final reel. The cinema, Lawrence Shaffer has reminded us, projects
a world of diminishing options: "[F]ilms run backward would blossom like flowers" (6). This entropic dimension of filmic narrative

FIGURE 1. *Jules and Jim*. Courtesy Jerry Ohlinger's

lends itself to an elegiac style: transposing the dominant musical score to a minor key or muting the color scheme, shifting from rapid cutting to sequence shots. Alternatively, the sense of lost energy may also be embodied in characterization through such theatrical and literary means as the actor's decreasing physical vitality, reversion to mechanical or compulsive behavior, or recession into memory or myth. Both Welles's Kane and Truffaut's Catherine exemplify how a character may embody not only the marks of diegetic time but also come to represent the irreversible, entropic nature of the film medium itself. Incomprehensible, exquisitely crafted, or emotionally moving passages in literature can be experienced or re-experienced at our own desired pace; the reader can delay—even infinitely postpone—the ending of a powerful novel. The power of a film, by contrast, necessarily dissipates into darkness, irrecoverable once the projector's energy has been turned off. And while the theater approximates this linear progression of events beyond the viewer's control, each staged performance, as Sontag suggests, becomes different from all others, "always new," as a result of the disparate energies of both actors and audience. Stage performers can wait for the laughter or applause to subside and can further acknowledge the spectators' influence in their curtain calls. Film, more like music, moves on despite the audience's desires.

REFLEXIVITY AND CHARACTER

In addition to evoking the spatial, temporal, and entropic qualities inherent in cinematic signification, many films more deliberately employ specific images or character types that suggest a relationship between the formal artifice of the movies and the equivocal nature of the characters they project. While the following assertion may be impossible to prove, it seems fair to say, for example, that a disproportionate percentage of those films that continue to attract the attention of serious viewers have been marked by the recurrence of privileged moments highlighting *mirrors* and *masks*. Less obviously than the reflexive use of movies-within-the-movie, these particular objects have served to remind us of the conditions under which all films are produced and consumed. Separated, screened from one another, filmmakers and spectators see their ideal self-conceptions as well as their darkest dreams reflected in the mirror and imperfectly concealed behind the mask.

David Bordwell warns against such "implicit" or "symptomatic" readings of a particular film's alleged reflexivity by cleverly illustrating the formulaic logic behind these interpretations, citing even his own well-known essay on *Citizen Kane* that compares the tension between reality and imagination to the cinema's historical split between the Lumières and Méliès. He concludes that "critics of all stripes have used virtually any means available to secure reflexive interpretations" and castigates "such an unconstrained extension of the concept" (Meaning 114–15). While one can readily agree that the mere presence of a mirror or mask within a movie is hardly a guarantee of its reflexivity (the *Friday the 13th* cycle immediately comes to mind), each example must be judged on its own merits. Surely Bordwell does not wish to confine the application of the concept to those relatively few movies whose diegetic world or explicit reference reflects the institution of film production and reception. In most cases cited here, the reflexive allusion seems intentional on the part of the filmmaker; in some instances, however, the connection may lie solely with the spectator trying to bring to consciousness the source of the image's suggestive effect.

Mirrors have been employed in countless commercial movies (*Lady from Shanghai*, *The Gambler*, all of the versions of *Dr. Jekyll and Mr. Hyde*) as well as art films (*Citizen Kane*, *Last Year at Marienbad*, *Persona*, *Paris, Texas*) to reflect the deceptive, artificial, and imaginary aspects of human identity and cinematic representation alike. Beyond foregrounding the figure of presence/absence previously described, such moments of mirror gazing seem to serve one of two purposes in relation to the film's protagonist: either to complicate our understanding of character through contemplating the double of an already ambiguous character or to confound our effort by presenting only the surface image of an irrevocably unknowable self. The depiction of Moreau's Catherine cited earlier may serve as an illustration of the first type, her face simultaneously immortal and time-bound, inviolate and "*très pathétique*," as Albert describes the slide of a sculpted woman displayed immediately before the statue Catherine is thought to resemble.

Another stunning representation of modern cinema's deconstruction of the notion of a coherent, integrated self may be found in the mirror shot that climaxes von Trotta's *Marianne and Juliane* (1982), a moment that also evokes the spectator's pursuit of the imaginary signifier. The journalist who, like Thompson in *Citizen Kane*, has become the spectator's diegetic surrogate in seeking knowledge about her terrorist sister, comes to visit Marianne in prison for what proves to be the last time. The scene's establishing shot configures the interview room as a movie theater: Juliane enters and takes her seat before a large rectangular window behind which the prisoner and her guards are carefully arranged. Following a sharply defined medium profile shot of Juliane, von Trotta cuts to an extraordinary close-up of Marianne, her face apparently distorted by the thick glass. "Your face is all blurred. I can't see it properly," her sister complains. Then through a subtle pan and Juliane's slight leaning to get a better view, the shot changes to two faces, revealing that we have been looking at Julie's reflection precisely superimposed on Marianne's face.[5] A new comprehension of the relation between these two apparently opposed sisters becomes clear: they are inextricably linked, twins in the deepest sense. Our recognition of presence/absence in this epiphany is immediately compounded by the failure of the microphone the sisters have been using to communicate, temporarily silencing Marianne's voice as the corrupt prison officials will soon permanently silence her. In the film's rather long denouement, Juliane will spend her life relentlessly yet fruitlessly pursuing the phantom double that has eluded her investigation.

Another kind of mirror shot can have precisely the opposite effect: to remind us of the cinema's status as a potentially empty signifier by revealing not a new meaning but simply another *image*. That is the interpretation most commentators have ascribed to the famous long shot of Kane infinitely duplicated in Xanadu's giant hallway mirror. A similar kind of pseudo-epiphany occurs at the end of Reisz's *The Gambler* (1974) when Axel Fried, bleeding from a stab wound across his face, glimpses his cloudy reflection in a Harlem hotel's mirror. The final freeze frame reveals nothing new about his character beyond confirmation of the pimp's frightened description of him moments earlier: "Mother fucker's *crazy!*" The mirror shots of Jake La Motta staring at his own image in *Raging Bull* (1980) may be even less definitive, expressing only the mystery he, like Travis Bickle in Scorsese's *Taxi Driver* (1976), has become to himself.

In a similar manner, masks can be made to project a disproportionately disturbing effect on audiences, even in genre pictures like *Escape from Alcatraz* (1979) or *The Taking of Pelham One Two Three* (1974), as well as in dozens of slasher movies in which their use is almost certainly not consciously reflexive. Nevertheless, the mask, more than any other object, does represent the cinema's unique *fort/da* appeal to the imaginary. When, in *Escape from Alcatraz*, we are startled by the papier-mâché head that rolls off the dummy the fleeing prisoner Frank Morris has left behind in his cell, it may be because the mask has replaced the face that had masked the character hidden behind it—Eastwood's famously impassive face, the actor himself a stand-in for the character now being impersonated on the screen by a two-dimensional image (fig. 2). In this singular case, all three figures—the actor, the prisoner in the diegesis, and the real Frank Morris—have been projected as fleeting: the first absent from the movie theater (leaving behind only his image), the second from the prison (leaving behind only his manufactured effigy), and the third from history (Frank's body, the movie's closing title informs us, having never been found).

This kind of "symptomatic" reading may send chills down David Bordwell's spine, but it seems at least as useful as invoking a cognitive schema to suggest how such an otherwise banal image haunts our memory of this generic text.[6] How else are we to explain the disturbing effect of such scenes as the one midway through Zinnemann's *The Day of the Jackal* (1973) when the sniper practicing to assassinate de Gaulle aims at a painted watermelon hanging from a distant tree? This sequence, in fact, may be studied in detail as a paradigm of the cinema's particular mode of representation at the same time that it conjures up the mystery of human identity.

THE TARGET PRACTICE SEQUENCE
IN *THE DAY OF THE JACKAL*

Like the more frequently discussed silent scene in Antonioni's *Blow Up* (1966) in which the photographer studies a succession of his enlargements, this sequence serves as the pivot on which Zinnemann's movie turns as well as the moment that most viewers are certain to remember. Both sections seem to lift the narratives at mid-point to another, more philosophical level by alluding to the phantom aspect of character and, by extension, the imaginary realm of the cinema itself. In *The Day of the Jackal*, the sequence begins when the would-be assassin, known as the Jackal (Edward Fox), takes his specially designed rifle to a bucolic meadow to fine tune the scope. Frederick Forsyth's original depiction of the scene in his novel—four pages in which the Jackal changes his clothes, paints the top and bottom of the melon brown and the center pink before adding the cartoon face, then fires nine shots before loading

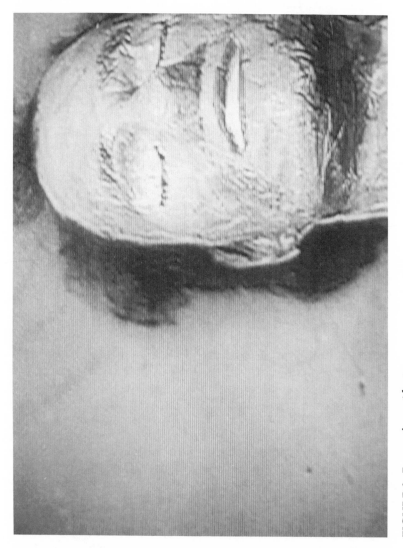

FIGURE 2. *Escape from Alcatraz*

the explosive bullet—lacks both the intensity and formal virtuosity of the film.

Consisting of seventeen shots in 135 seconds, Zinnemann's tour de force serves most obviously to anticipate the intended result of the conspirators' plot and to define the cold-hearted precision of the professional assassin. In terms of narrative trajectory, it both culminates the Jackal's various preparations and initiates the execution of his plans; moreover, as a rehearsal for the film's aborted climax, it satisfies the audience's desire to see, at least in symbolic form, the ultimate act of violence denied in this case by history. In addition to these diegetic functions, the target practice sequence also works in intertextual and reflexive ways to fix our attention on a lost object destroyed before our eyes.

The framing long shots that begin and end the sequence may be used to measure the dimensions of the Jackal's disruption of the natural order. Shot #1 establishes the picturesque landscape, the tree centered at the vanishing point of a perfectly balanced composition (fig. 3). Shot #17 is a reverse long shot, the melon hanging in front of the camera in the upper part of the frame, then exploding in a burst of red as the test bullet finds its target, destroying the fruit of this lost paradise (fig. 4). The shocking impact stems in part from this violation of the harmonious visual design, which had been reinforced by the peaceful chirping of birds, but also from the reverse angle, which directs the assault not simply against the melon, but against us, who have been carefully positioned in the line of fire.

The second shot, a close-up of the Jackal painting a crude face on the melon, identifies the symbolic identity of the target as Charles de Gaulle. In effect, the melon becomes a mask, one seen again through the crosshairs of the rifle scope in four successive masking shots (#s 9, 11, 13, and 15). The cartooned surface now signifies a de Gaulle who is absent from the diegetic scene, absent from the film (subsequently impersonated from long range by a virtually anonymous French actor [Adrien Cayla]), and absent from the real present (deceased two years before the film's production).

The last three masking shots in the sequence (#s 11, 13, and 15) depict the mask, shot. The stylized, generic form of this particular representation—a target carefully aligned through a rifle's telescopic sight—implies the unseen presence of a third elusive character beyond the frame: not the Jackal (who has adopted the name of a long-deceased child, Paul Oliver Duggan, and who travels on

FIGURE 3. *The Day of the Jackal*

FIGURE 4. *The Day of the Jackal*

FIGURE 5. *The Day of the Jackal*

twenty-three different passports, one of which belongs to Charles
Harold Calthrop, the man being pursued by the French police) and
not Charles de Gaulle, but rather the director, Fred Zinnemann
(fig. 5). The analogy between the sniper's activity and the filmmaker's has been inscribed here both by the Jackal's meticulous
adjustments after each practice shot—or "take"—seen in tight
close-ups in shots #10, 12, and 14, and by the camera's own fidgety
zooms in shot #5, when he hangs the melon on a branch, and at the
end of shot #6, when he first sights the target. Zinnemann's awareness of this reflexive relation has been memorialized in a special
photograph he had taken at the time, showing his own head posed
in profile in front of the melon and between the crosshairs of the
scope along with the caption: "I wonder if someone would have
liked to pull the trigger" (Zinnemann 219).

The final shot in the sequence—the melon exploding in front of
the camera, the now empty air it had occupied suspended by Zinnemann for an extra second—extends our sense of its status as a "lost
object" within the cinema's imaginary scopic regime. Shot #17 thus
offers an unusually elaborate matrix of presence/absence (fig. 6).

FIGURE 6. *The Day of the Jackal*

1. the melon itself, like all filmed images, not really present at the time of projection just as the spectator has not been present at the time of shooting;
2. the Jackal, present in the extreme distance, literally beyond the vanishing point, but not visible in the long shot that records the ultimate effect of his experiment;
3. de Gaulle, absent from the scene, absent from life, but represented in effigy by the painted melon;
4. the painted face on the melon, not really a caricature of de Gaulle or any other human face but an abstraction, now turned away from the camera, concealed from the spectator's vision by the reverse angle, for the only time in the sequence;
5. the spatial and aural emptiness (the muffled impact of the bullet, the silence of the birds) that follows the melon's destruction, leaving behind only a vestigial fragment of fruit dangling from the mesh bag that once held it.[7]

In a broader sense, Zinnemann's film addresses the basic mystery of character that the cinema, as we have suggested, seems especially well suited to portray. Thus reviewers like the one from *Newsweek* who complained that the assassin's "motives and outlook are never explored, his background and personality do not exist" (P. D. Z. 101) have missed the metaphorical implication of the exploding melon. Ultimately, *The Day of the Jackal* reminds viewers of the transience as well as the fragility of identity when, in the epilogue, the true name of "the Jackal," himself assassinated, remains a mystery he takes to the grave.

PHANTOM TYPES

In the same way as most movies use stereotypes to establish and fix character, reflexive films may often employ variants of a cipher figure like the Jackal—incarnations of the double, the spy, the undercover agent, or the confidence man—to echo in the diegesis the operation of its own signifying apparatus. Leo Braudy has explored this meta-cinematic aspect in such films as Hitchcock's *Shadow of a Doubt* (1943):

> The double is only an important subtheme in the body of nineteenth-century literature. In film it has been the most prevalent way of defining human nature. The double expresses

in terms of theme and plot something of the inner aesthetic of films, the double exposure, the fleeting insubstantiality of the image, its potential lack of authority even at the moment of greatest assertion. This simultaneous reality and transience of the film image can imply that character itself, so palpably before you, is merely a construction. (227)

A thorough taxonomy of these character types together with close analysis of various illustrations remains beyond the scope of this project, although subsequent chapters should provide an indication of the potential value in such a study. For now, Braudy's observation may be substantiated by briefly citing connections between elusive characters and the cinema's "inner aesthetic" in depictions of the double in Mamoulian's and Fleming's sound versions of *Dr. Jekyll and Mr. Hyde* (1932, 1941; the use of "special effects" to transform March's and Tracy's faces largely replacing the theatrical histrionics of Barrymore's performance in the silent predecessor) or the cipher in such different movies as *Being There* (1979; the out-takes during the closing credits that reveal a giddy Peter Sellers rehearsing his role as the phlegmatic Chance), *Zelig* (1983; the pseudo-documentary footage representing the Chameleon Man in a series of uncanny appearances), and *In the Line of Fire* (1993; the digitalized transfigurations of the would-be assassin projected on a computer screen).

As we shall see, Ingmar Bergman has persistently explored the doppelganger theme, most notably in *The Magician* (1958) and *Persona* (1966), through deceptive avatars of the artist (often named "Vogler") in order to probe the mutually degrading, latently hostile relationship between exhibitionist/actor and voyeur/audience. In these model texts of the art cinema, Bergman deliberately questions the artist's potential both to deceive and to redeem by foregrounding his own manipulation of the medium we have come to trust and, especially in the case of a "Bergman film," to worship. *The Cabinet of Dr. Caligari* (1919) provides another example of how a classic film text engages in a complex form of self-inquiry (problematizing both *a* self within the diegesis and *itself* as a recording of objective reality), beginning with the inscription of presence/absence through the narrative frame. Whether the storyteller is taken to be Francis or the doctor, neither character appears within the tale in anything like the ambiguous form he takes at the end: Francis lost in madness, Caligari shrouded in mystery. The monster, Cesare, seems at first sight hardly frightening but merely a rather tall, skinny young man in black tights. His phantom character emanates instead from his stylized makeup (his face in close-up resembling a mask) and somnambulistic movements, together signifying a personality and will now surrendered to another's control. Caligari's tyranny thus parallels the filmmaker's (and that of Bergman's Voglers), a doubling suggested first in his seduction of the carnival crowd by setting up a screen outside his tent and ultimately in his claim that the horrific tale the spectator has witnessed was only an illusion, the projection of his patient's paranoid imagination.

Partially in response to the pressure caused by the cinema's stronger claims to verisimilitude in addition to a variety of cultural and historical conditions, twentieth-century literature underwent the kind of revolution Tolstoy had anticipated, turning with greater frequency to the kind of slippery characters and reflexive strategies we have been describing. Following the arrival of sound and the apparent triumph of naturalism through the hegemony of the classical Hollywood cinema, many foreign art films, following the novel's lead, took on a modernist cast by deliberately subverting their own capacity to render seamless narrative (*Last Year at Marienbad*, 1961), surface action (*L'Avventura*, 1960), and objective truth (*Rashomon*, 1950). Contemporary literary and film theory, with its emphasis on sliding signifiers, deconstruction, and indeterminacy, has further undermined confidence in the efficacy of Hollywood's formulaic depictions of readily comprehensible characters. Thus, the representation of persons like Catherine in *Jules and Jim*, Elisabet Vogler in *Persona*, even the Jackal among mainstream American movies, along with the protagonists in a myriad of modern films to be discussed later in this book, has come to function as a kind of synecdoche for cinema itself.

As a quintessential postmodernist text, *Reservoir Dogs* (1992) constructs the phantom of character in its most recent permutation. The characters in Tarantino's first feature are identified only by colors ("Mr. Orange," "Mr. Pink," etc.) or by monikers like "Nice Guy Eddie." As if lifted from a structuralist's diagram, they truly exist only as agents of a plot that deconstructs the familiar caper film. In what can stand as the paradigmatic Tarantino shot, Mr. Orange, an undercover cop (otherwise known only as "Freddie") who has infiltrated the "colorful" gang, is depicted in long shot against a brilliant graffiti-painted wall, his chameleon character totally adapted to his surroundings so that he is virtually indistinguishable from the chaotic background, himself the very image

FIGURE 7. *Reservoir Dogs*

of an empty signifier (fig. 7). While Leonard Zelig had embodied modernism's prevailing view of character as a lost wholeness, alienated from society, Mr. Orange here perfectly represents postmodernism's preference for spectacle over meaning, flatness over depth.

CITIZEN KANE

As all philosophy can be described as having begun with Plato, all film criticism seems to begin with *Citizen Kane*. Welles's celebrated work serves to close the argument here because it remains one of the first and most compelling films of the modern era to focus on the problematic task of representing a unified, coherent, and discoverable sense of personhood. Noting that it calls to mind genre conventions it often deliberately undermines, Bordwell has described how "*Citizen Kane* becomes a mystery story; but instead of investigating a crime, the reporter investigates a character" (Film Art 78). In several important ways, *Citizen Kane* compounds the complexity of its protagonist by exploiting the dimension of presence/absence as it has been previously defined.

Little needs to be added, of course, to the countless analyses of Welles's meta-cinematic representation of Kane: the aforementioned mirrored reflection in the hallway at Xanadu, for example, receding into infinity, or his silhouette projecting animal images on the wall of Susan's flat, both moments interrupting the narrative to confirm the audience's position as spectators and at the same time to crystallize their perception of the protagonist as both image and image maker. We might pause, however, to consider the less celebrated instance of presence/absence when the trapped candidate bellows an empty threat at his departing political rival: "Don't worry about me, Geddes! Don't worry about me! I'm *Charles Foster Kane!*" Welles signifies the hollowness of Kane's assertion of his own powerful identity through a sound bridge to the horn of an unseen car blaring in the empty street below. In something like the way in which the office ceiling viewed from a low angle undercuts the looming presence of the defeated Kane in his post-election dialogue with Leland, the absent horn nullifies his loud insistence on his personal integrity ("I'm no cheap politician!"), the off-screen signifier undermining his claim to autonomy.

In addition to its portrayal of Kane himself, *Citizen Kane* constructs the phantom of character through the figures of Thompson, "Rosebud," and the film's tail credits. Thompson has generally been regarded as a surrogate for the spectator, a shadowy double sharing the viewer's position in darkness during the search for the meaning of Kane's life. But he is also a figure of the cinematic signifier, a presence of absence existing in a "primordial elsewhere," not so much *in* the movie as *of* the movies. Indeed, Thompson embodies each of the three aspects of loss inherent to film's process of signification. First and most obviously, he is spatially distanced from Kane, absent from all the events of Kane's life (shooting) and present only when Kane is absent, most conspicuously in the projection room. A kind of obverse reflection of Kane himself, he comes to represent not the overabundance of detail—the excess of spectacle—but the very *lack* that stimulates spectatorial desire (like Rosebud, the object of his own quest). Moreover, and particularly important in differentiating Thompson from the film spectator, he also absents himself when the significance of the sled is revealed. Like the Jackal, he remains a cipher, without even a first name (unless we listen extremely attentively to the rapid-fire reporters' dialogue) or personal history, seen almost exclusively in shadow, barely more substantial than the silhouettes Kane had cast on Susan's wall.

Thompson's distance from Kane is also temporal, not just because of the years that separate them but because of the styles of journalism they represent. Just as the "News on the March" traces the evolution of documentary filmmaking, so Thompson reflects the emergent form of print journalism—newsweeklies like *Time*—that helped drive many newspapers (as well as the newsreels) out of business. Kane himself confronts this new kind of reporter, his modern double, when he jauntily chides the radio interviewer in the newsreel clip: "Come on, young fella. In my day we asked 'em quicker than that!" More than fifty years later, of course, such images as the huge microphone or the newsreel's bombastic narration have become suffused with their own historicity. And while Thompson may exemplify the latest fashion in investigative reporting, he remains no less vulnerable to passing time: thus, his inquiry is initially compromised by Rawlston's deadline and, in the concluding diegetic sequence, by the train he must catch. Finally, his sigh of exhaustion at the end of the search duplicates the entropic feel of the camera's slow crane shot over the detritus of Xanadu, the inanimate signifier of a lost and largely wasted life. Like its protagonist, *Citizen Kane* dissipates its narrative energy once the *Inquirer* party is over, later echoing Charlie's exuberant song in a minor key and parodying his graceful dance as if weighted down by the effort of self-construction.

The most celebrated of the film's images, the Rosebud sled, along with the glass ball seen shattered in the opening sequence and subsequently recovered as a "lost object" on Susan's dressing table, effectively symbolizes the melancholy of an irrecoverable past and the eternal mystery of Kane's character—or anyone's, as Thompson reminds us in his exit line. Michael Wood has suggested how its meaning derives more from the manner of signification—the expressive detail consumed only moments after it has finally been perceived—than from the object's status as a thematic signifier:

> [T]he sight of the name disappearing in the fire . . . doesn't seem sentimental, or overly ironic, it feels thoroughly distressing, not because the answer has been found too late, but because it has been lost as soon as it has been found. The world of the visible has yielded its prime clue, but the clue scarcely stayed long enough for us to read it: a title card in a silent movie, taken away almost too soon. (125)

The sled's immolation at the end of *Citizen Kane* thus parallels the shattering of the glass globe at the beginning, its consignment to the furnace ultimately negating the camera's discovery just as the earlier close-up of the glass ball being dropped has nullified Kane's apparent rescue of it after he destroys Susan's room. In the film's climactic vision of consumption, the camera's revelation of what Kracauer would term the redemption of physical reality transforms Rosebud into the incarnation of Metz's lost object, invoked and revoked almost simultaneously. As an index of Kane's character, Rosebud may indeed be "dollar book Freud," as Welles admitted, but as an image of the endless desire for an irretrievable ideal, this moment does fulfill the spectator's quest for some profound truth. The search that Rawlston initiates for "'Rosebud,' dead or alive!" ends with Rosebud dead *and* alive.

Before the film itself is totally consumed and winds off the sprockets, *Citizen Kane* adds an extra-diegetic reminder of the relation between its phantom protagonist and the play of presence/absence in the cinematic signifier. At first glance, the tail credits might seem a superfluous, theatrical flourish in which the Mercury Theatre performers take their bows. The images themselves appear at first to be outtakes from the movie just completed, lost moments re-enacted in a kind of nostalgic curtain call. Instead, the careful viewer will recognize that none of these shots has been taken from the text of *Citizen Kane*:

> These visual tail credits constitute pieces of a rough draft
> designed by the implied author to reveal for the last time his
> strategy of betrayed expectations. We may infer from them the
> existence of not only other Kanes but other *Kanes* . . . by not
> including Welles/Kane. The absence of Kane and the reprise of
> that rousing campaign song with its interrogative lyrics signal
> for one last time Kane's elusiveness. Where is Kane? Who is
> that man? These two implied and unanswered questions, part
> of our experience of the film's last moments, suspend, indefi-
> nitely, our closing on *Citizen Kane*. (Leff 19–20)

As the tail credits thus conjure up a series of details missing from
the film proper, they also exclude the dominant presence within
Citizen Kane of Charles Foster Kane himself (or Orson Welles,
whose presence is signified only by his printed name). One last
time the film reflects the fundamental dialectic of presentation and
withdrawal that constitutes the cinema's particular way of sum-
moning forth the ungraspable phantom of life that Melville con-
cluded was "the key to it all."

The value of the paradigm of presence/absence as a touch-
stone for the analysis of characterization in specific films may
now be summarized as essentially threefold: (1) it helps to define
how certain films delineate the indeterminacy of character by
employing the unique properties of the cinema's signifying practice; (2) it provides a credible account for the prominence of certain character types (ghosts, monsters, spies, ciphers, doubles,
confidence men) and narrative modes (elegiac, pornographic) and
illuminates their reflexive aspect; (3) it offers a partial explanation
for the endurance of certain classic works through their construction of character as a lost object, thereby replenishing spectatorial
desire.

At the same time, we need to remind ourselves that most
films attempt to overcome their inherent fictionality just as novelists and playwrights commonly do, by assigning to characters
familiar, stable signifiers. Thus, for every *House of Games* (1987),
there may be a score of more accessible pictures like *The Sting*
(1973); for every *Reilly: Ace of Spies* (1984), a dozen James Bond
thrillers; for every *The Crying Game* (1992), numerous *Tootsies*
(1982). But the commercial constraints of mainstream moviemaking should not inhibit attempts to explain the lasting appeal of
either such transcendent moments as von Bulow's reply to Der-

showitz's assertion of his monumental strangeness—"You have no idea!"—or such exceptional cinematic texts as those that will be explored in the rest of this book, films redolent with otherwise inexpressible truths about the mystery of human identity and the "inner aesthetic" of film art.

CHAPTER TWO

◆

Reflexivity and Character in Persona

Ingmar Bergman's *Persona* provides an ideal starting point for illustrating the phantom quality of film character proposed in the introduction. Originally called simply "Film" or "Kinematography" before Svensk Filmindustri insisted on a more appealing title, *Persona* continually reminds us of its constructed, artificial status while at the same time deconstructing our conventional conception of character as unified and coherent. It provoked respectful if puzzled reviews following its 1966 release and subsequently elicited a series of hermeneutical essays in scholarly journals and books.[8] Today it is generally regarded as Bergman's masterpiece and one of the canonical texts of the modern cinema.

Undoubtedly much of the mystique that has developed about *Persona* stems from the film's apparent opacity. No less a Bergman authority than Peter Cowie has declared, somewhat hyperbolically, "Everything one says about *Persona* may be contradicted; the opposite will also be true" (231). Inverting Metz's celebrated aphorism about the legibility of most movies, we might say that *Persona* has proven to be easy to talk about because it is difficult to understand. Nevertheless, most discussions of the film to date, having once agreed on its tantalizing ambiguity (thereby valorizing their own efforts at explanation), share the view that, whatever else it may be about, *Persona* is concerned with the problematic aspects of character—seen as doubled or split, parasitic or neurotic, protean or antiheroic—and of film itself. "*Persona* is not just a respresentation of transactions between the two characters, Alma and Elizabeth,"

33

Susan Sontag explains, "but a meditation on the film which is 'about' them" (*Radical Will*, 136). My discussion will concentrate on these two most conspicuous themes, seeking first to define more rigorously than in previous accounts precisely how *Persona* becomes self-referential and then to suggest how this reflexivity reinforces the mystery of character implied by the film's title.

THE IMAGINARY SIGNIFIER

As we have shown, the element of presence/absence inscribed by the cinema's system of signification can help to account for the recurrence of such phantom figures as the double, the spectre, and the vampire, each of which is evoked in *Persona*. Metz has termed this distinctive mode of filmic representation "the imaginary signifier":

> For it is the signifier itself, and as a whole, that is recorded, that is absence: a little rolled up perforated strip which "contains" vast landscapes, fixed battles, the melting of ice on the River Neva, and whole lifetimes, and yet can be enclosed in the familiar round metal tin, of modest dimensions, clear proof that it does not "really" contain all that. (Imaginary 43–44)

Cinema thus always presents us with a "double withdrawal" measured by our distance from the screened object in the theater and by the delegated image of absent objects.

> Characteristic of the cinema is not the imaginary that it may happen to represent, it is the imaginary that it *is* from the start, the imaginary that constitutes it as a signifier. . . . In the cinema it is not just the fictional signified, if there is one, that is thus made present in the mode of absence, it is from the outset the signifier.
> Thus the cinema, "more perceptual" than certain arts according to the list of its sensory registers, is also "less perceptual" than others once the status of these perceptions is envisaged rather than their number or diversity: for its perceptions are all in a sense "false." Or rather, the activity of perception in it is not real (the cinema is not a fantasy), but the perceived is not really the object, it is its shade, its phantom, its *double*. (44–45)

While Metz describes here the generic "object" that cinema represents in every instance (travelogue, industrial film, archival documentary, home movie as well as fictional narrative), his theory applies in particular ways to character, which is always imagined, always constructed from surface evidence that remains necessarily incomplete despite film's obvious advantages over other art forms in rendering the human figure with convincing and flexible detail. Unlike filmed settings, which are either fabricated to be transient in the case of studio sets or which remain permanently present in the case of location shooting, characters—in film as in life—are "phantoms" with respect to the bundle of traits that are given and the infinite galaxy of unknown characteristics that are withheld. Thus, Rick's Cafe never actually functioned as a gin mill in Casablanca, any more than Nurse Alma's introduction to Elisabet Vogler took place in a working hospital; on the other hand, Mt. Rushmore remains essentially unchanged from the time when Cary Grant visited there, just as Faro Island is much the same as when Liv Ullmann and Bibi Andersson acted in *Persona*.

   While Metz's formulation of "the imaginary signifier" is both derivative (from Bazin's comparison of film and theater as well as Lacan's analysis of "the mirror phase") and now somewhat dated, and while it has been critiqued as both patriarchal and ahistorical, his thesis concerning how the cinema's play of presence/absence creates desire in the spectator for the filmed image as "lost object" remains a credible, useful formula for discussing a work like *Persona*. But because Metz has confined himself to a psychoanalytical model and because he writes almost exclusively as a theorist, the value of his work for illuminating the powerful hold of certain film characters has remained largely unexplored. My interest in invoking it throughout this study is not primarily to buttress a psychoanalytic reading of fictional characters (which risks treating them as if they were real, a critical approach that seems both tenuous at best in light of any cinematic text's limited access to their personal histories, unspoken thoughts, and subconscious impulses and more tempting for a relatively naturalistic Bergman film like *Face to Face* [1976]); instead, I want to explore "a certain tendency" within modern, post-Hollywood cinema to represent characters as simultaneously vivid and evanescent, compelling and elusive, resonant and inexpressible. In doing so, I hope to attend to both the structuralist appeal to character as a formal narrative convention and the humanist interest in character as analogous to persons encountered in life.

The very first sustained action in *Persona*, the pre-credit sequence in which a boy gazes at, then reaches out to touch the shifting projected still image of a woman's face, suggests the potential connection between this film's pervasive reflexivity and its presentation of character. In addition to Metz's distinction between the cinema and the theater, however, we need to keep in mind Barthes's contrast between the photograph, in which something has *posed* before the camera, and film, in which something has *passed* (Camera 82).[9] Thus, the still image of Ullmann/Andersson continually changes, moving in and out of focus as well as fading from one face to the other, so as to avoid identification. Following this prologue, *Persona* continues to explore its own nature as an imaginary signifier through successive permutations of what can be termed a *triple* withdrawal: Metz's distance from the screen together with the delegated image of absent objects, *plus* an image that is withdrawn, interrupted, destroyed, or obscured before it can become a fully comprehensible signified. Specifically, *Persona* presents at least nine syntagmatic units alluding to presence of absence. Each of these moments involves a different medium of communication that becomes associated through its mode of presentation with the cinema's unique system of signification. Frequently, for example, the key images are illuminated by a concentrated source of light analogous to the film projector, or the mise-en-scène imitates the viewing situation in the movie theater. In chronological order and stripped of all but their syntagmatic function, these units include:

1. An enlarged still projection of a woman's face is seen to fade, to reappear, to shift focus, and to return transformed.
2. A theatrical role is interrupted.
3. A radio play is switched off.
4. A television newsreel depicting self-immolation is narrated in a foreign language, then silenced.
5. A family snapshot is torn in half.
6. A letter is intercepted.
7. A segment of film splits in half and is burned.
8. An historical photograph depicting mass arrests is removed from a book and propped under a table lamp.
9. A film projector ceases to project.

In addition to these privileged moments of reflexivity, *Persona*'s much-admired opening sequence preceding and including the credits also serves to foreground the film's production and mode of enunciation. Essential to the problematic referentiality of these gnomic images is the rapidity of their presentation, their refusal, in Barthes's term, to *pose*. The shots in the credit sequence pass by as virtually subliminal perceptions; those in the pre-credit series (except for the boy looking at the woman's face) depend for their signification upon other images that are conspicuously absent, either the shots that precede and follow (as in Kuleshov's famous experiment with montage) or the ones that may exist in our mind's anthology of other films (as in Simon's interpretation of the sequence as a recapitulation of Bergman's film career). For example, the long shot of bare ground with a hole to the left, an iron gate in the foreground, and a building in the background is commonly understood to signify an open grave because it follows separate close-ups of hands, eyes, entrails, and immediately precedes still shots of aged faces. Or, to illustrate the second case, the close-up of a spider is taken to refer to Bergman's evocation of the spider god in *Through a Glass Darkly* (1962).The editing technique applied so prominently throughout *Persona*'s opening sequence, absenting images before they can be assimilated into some comprehensible psychological or intellectual order, thus affirms before we enter the diegetic realm that the spectator (like the boy who, having turned his back to assume our viewing position, also resumes his gaze out at us) searches for an object that has become lost, that is not really there.

The transition from credits to diegesis occurs when the screen goes entirely white, absenting all images, before it becomes the hospital wall of the narrative's opening scene. While Elisabet's doctor explains the patient's case to Sister Alma, Bergman intercuts a tight shot of Mrs. Vogler performing as Electra. This image of *a theatrical role being interrupted* again subtly alludes to the cinematic signifier: the actress slowly turns away from the intense stage lamps prominent in the background and looks directly into the camera (fig. 8). For a striking instant, she appears simultaneously projected by the bright light "behind" as well as in front of the screen. Her heavy stage make-up, reminiscent in its dark, patently false disguise of her namesake and fellow silent actor, Albert Emanuel Vogler in Bergman's *The Magician*, signifies an as yet unknown, absent identity.

Soon after she first visits Elisabet in her hospital room, Alma turns her patient's radio on to a domestic melodrama. After giggling contemptuously at the hammy performance, Elisabet suddenly *switches off the radio*. The medium shot Bergman maintains

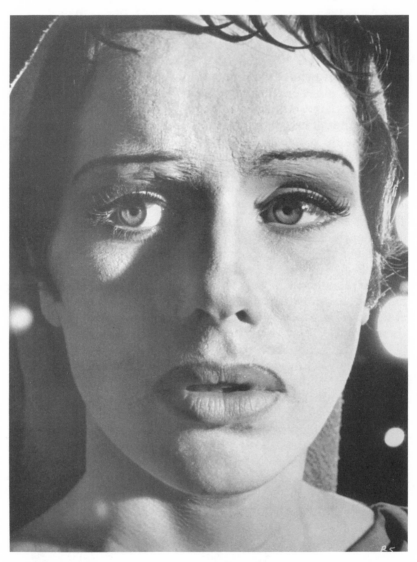

FIGURE 8. *Persona*. Courtesy Museum of Modern Art

throughout this scene evokes once more the circumstances of film projection. The radio sits in the foreground, turned away from the camera so that its most prominent detail is the glowing tube that illuminates Elisabet's face in the midst of darkness. This composition is complemented by a subsequent scene in which Elisabet stares horrified at *a television newsreel recording the self-immolation* of a Buddhist monk (fig. 9). Although the bonze's protest conveys a powerful immediacy, the aural-visual elements of this film-within-the-film also involve an equal measure of withdrawal and distance. By virtue of its being narrated, the event already belongs to the past (and to *Persona*'s audience has become a part of history). Moreover, the distance separating Elisabet's Swedish hospital room from the spectacle in Vietnam is furthered by the reporter's narration in English, a fact compounded by the patient's retreat to a far corner of the room, creating the scene's closing long shot in which the television set (like the radio) is placed so that its light but not its picture is visible. Bergman holds this image—television in the extreme right foreground of the frame, Mrs. Vogler cringing in the left background—long enough to suggest that the television has become, in effect, a projector casting Elisabet's shadow on the white wall. As if to reinforce the reflexive allusion, the transmission is interrupted this time not by Elisabet turning the switch, but by a direct cut to silence and the absence of light glowing from the television screen. As he will most conspicuously in the voiceover narration that describes the women's initially harmonious relationship on the island, Bergman intervenes to bring about the transition.

While still at the hospital, Alma hesitantly reads to her patient a letter from Mr. Vogler containing a photograph of her son. Elisabet abruptly *rips the snapshot in half*, exactly as the film itself will later split vertically down the middle. Later too, this same photograph, strangely repaired, will be deliberately concealed beneath Elisabet's hands—made absent despite its presence in the shot—until Alma reveals it and begins her famous twice-told monologue describing Mrs. Vogler's failed motherhood. None of the roles Elisabet adopts-then-abandons during *Persona*—"actress," "patient," "wife," "mother"—proves sufficient to contain her.

Many critics have identified the scene in which Alma *intercepts a letter* from Elisabet to her doctor as the turning point in their relationship, but without noticing how Bergman's presentation again inscribes reflexive elements in its formal design. This time, neither the letter's author nor the intended audience is present as

40

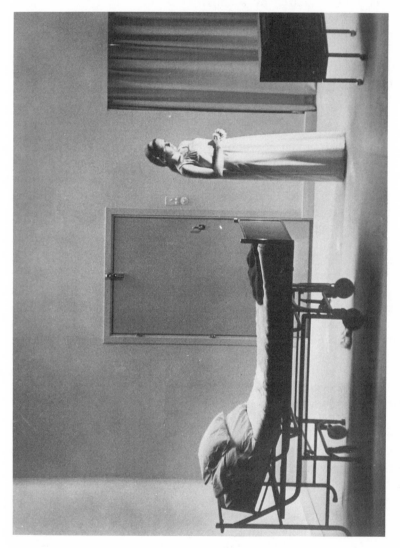

FIGURE 9. *Persona*. Courtesy Museum of Modern Art

Alma sits alone in the Volvo reading it. The close-up of this now lost object deserves attention. The fact that the letter is typewritten signifies both the writer's emotional detachment as she "studies" her subject, Alma, and this particular film's prior means of identifying its own dramatis personae—the names in stark type against a white background seen in *Persona*'s credits. Bergman seems conscious of the connection to his own authorship here: thus, the magnified lines of typescript in the letter are viewed in isolation, a single line at a time, the surrounding frame entirely white.[10]

Shortly after this pivotal sequence and as a result of the tension it creates, *the film appears to rip down its center and burn out to whiteness*. The rapidly intercut images from the pre-credit sequence that follow simultaneously re-present earlier imperfectly assimilated material (a devil, a comic movie, a spike driven through a bleeding hand) and absent the diegetic narrative that up to this moment has so intensely engaged us. As the figure of a woman at first deeply in shadow and out of focus gradually re-emerges, the film suddenly snaps into sharp focus, artificially restoring the spectator's relation to the lost object, *Persona*.

The most complex of these moments when the film seems to reflect upon its own status as an imaginary signifier begins with *an historical photograph Elisabet has concealed in a book*. The hiding place both prefigures Elisabet's effort to conceal her child's snapshot from Alma and, along with Lermontov's novel glimpsed in the pre-credits and the two letters in the diegesis, confirms the ontological distinction between print and film. The celebrated photograph depicts Nazi mass arrests in the Warsaw ghetto; a small boy with his hands in the air and an expression of bewildered fear stands in the foreground, "a photo-souvenir of the essence of tragedy" (Sontag, Photography 109). Like the bonze in the newsreel, he has been photographed as he is about to be destroyed.[11] As permanently lost figures, the boy and the monk are now not merely "elsewhere," but *nowhere*. The way in which Elisabet contemplates the photograph again suggests an analogy to the cinema's projector and screen: the picture is carefully propped upright under a table lamp that serves as a kind of easel and provides the single source of light in the darkened room (fig. 10). As if to reinforce the association, Bergman fragments the image through a montage sequence, thereby foregrounding the narrational device that remains so central to cinematic art.

In *Persona*'s closing moments, *a film projector ceases to project*. Even this direct reference to the film apparatus employs the

FIGURE 10. *Persona*

paradigm of presence of absence when the viewer recognizes, as Frank D. McConnell has noted, "If the light *were* turned off, we would not see the footage of the arc light *being* turned off" (36). McConnell sees this fact as an artistic weakness because it "violates our experience of the film's photographic realism" without appreciating how it inscribes for a final time a unique aspect of the cinema's mode of signification: in this case, the discrepancy between the absent object's delegated image and the projector that is still present and projecting in the auditorium. Only when *that* projector ceases to function are we freed—at least partially—from the hold of the film's imaginary order.

THE NECESSARY ILLUSION

At the risk of pedantry, I have belabored the formalist analysis of *Persona*'s richly detailed, persistent reflexivity in order to account for the film's success in projecting the uncanny even while it constructs a mimetic narrative throughout the middle section concerned with the evolving relationship between two women. The motif of presence/absence, in fact, can be observed in several other scenes—the night visit to Alma's bedroom that Elisabet denies the next day; the long shot that depicts Elisabet stepping on a shard of glass only after Alma, who had deliberately left it there, absents herself from the area; the two moments when Elisabet is heard to speak (telling Alma to go to sleep, later screaming "Don't!" when she is threatened with boiling water) without actually being seen; the closing montage in which Elisabet can be glimpsed out of make-up and upside down in the movie camera's viewfinder immediately after she was seen in performance as Electra—where it suggests the interplay of distance and imagination that underlies every cinematic experience. But Alan Barr is quite right in arguing "that it is not the framing sequences and the cinematic pyrotechnics that impress us most, but what occurs between Alma and Elisabet" (126). Their story, nevertheless, is closely related to the film's startling formal qualities, as Barr and others have observed.

In her influential essay on *Persona*, Susan Sontag has proposed that the film's construction might best be understood as variations on the theme of doubling (Radical Will 135), a description that squares both with Metz's definition of the cinematic signifier's "dual character" (perceptual wealth plus unreality) and Braudy's observations about the how the doppelganger reflects the "simultaneous reality and transience of the film image." Bergman under-scores the doubling of character through numerous mirror shots—most notably the long take of Alma's figure reflected in the pond after she reads Elisabet's letter and the repeated image of Elisabet pulling back Alma's hair to display their resemblance—leading to the terrifying fusion of the protagonists' faces following Alma's doubled monologue. On the point of breakdown, the nurse cries out, "No, I am not Elisabet Vogler! I am Sister Alma!" Her verbal protest asserts an autonomous identity that the image repudiates first through a nearly subliminal cut in which her face appears to split in half. Moments later, when her speech concludes in the famous trick shot, the spectator confronts a "new" character—or rather, a new mask—that is actually no character and is never seen again. The film's great triumph at this instant lies in having trans-formed two beautiful actresses into the single image of a monster.

When we consider its historical references to the Holocaust and Vietnam as well as its re-figuring of the women's faces into the climactic image of a monstrous double, *Persona* may be fairly regarded as a modernist horror movie. In its other film-within-a-film, in fact, *Persona* (twice) includes a snippet of primitive horror farce in which a man is chased around his bedroom by a skeleton, a scene Bergman first used in *Prison* (1949). While nearly all horror films involving aliens or monsters are versions of the doppelganger, *Persona* specifically evokes the vampire genre through its images of Elisabet lowering her head to caress the nape of Alma's neck and later sucking the blood that bubbles from her wrist. In addition, Alma's dedication to caring for others, her breakdown into madness and violence, and her attraction to mirrors all conjure up the phan-tom of Dr. Jekyll/Mr. Hyde.

The film's title, of course, introduces the motif of masks that culminates in the "special effects" close-up of Alma/Elisabet—a mask, to borrow Barthes's description of modern art, pointing to itself. As *Persona* problematizes narrative representation and con-tinuity in its formal design, its diegesis blurs conventional distinc-tions between being and role-playing. Elisabet's psychiatrist explic-itly states the theme in her diagnosis:

> Don't you think I understand? The hopeless dream to *be*. Not seem but be. Conscious and watchful every second. And at the same time the abyss between what you are to others and what you are to yourself . . . I understand your refusal to speak, your immobility, your making will-lessness into a fantastic sys-

tem. I understand and I admire. I believe you will hold on to this role until you find it uninteresting, played out, and you can drop it as, one by one, you've dropped all your others.

Because the doctor's clinical opinion is addressed directly to the audience and seems borne out by the narrative's conclusion, many commentators have taken her analysis to represent, more or less, Bergman's view of the existentialist dilemma and its ultimate resolution. Such a reading must be qualified, however, not only by the speech's placement so early in the narrative, never to be repeated or alluded to, but by the psychiatrist's detached, authoritarian, and imperious demeanor as she pronounces the verdict of science. In her anonymity and subsequent disengagement, she too wears a mask. In Bergman's other films (*The Magician*, *The Passion of Anna*, *The Touch* [1971]), her name is Vergérus.

The hopeless dream of being, *Persona* implies, is the shared condition of both life and film art. In its aspiration to escape subjectivity, the cinema inevitably falls back on its special effects and the audience's willing suspension of disbelief; in our desire to live in truth, we invariably resort to another kind of performance that reality will, in time, unmask. "It's all a tissue of lies" (*Cries and Whispers*). But to go beyond Romantic conceptions of the artist as redeeming visionary or exemplary sufferer, as Elisabet apparently has, or to renounce a conventional life of service, as Alma seemingly does, need not necessitate dismissing the efficacy of either works of art or good deeds. To the tyranny of lies, Bergman responds with the necessity of illusions.

Paisley Livingston approaches the view that I think *Persona*—and the body of Ingmar Bergman's work—ultimately upholds when he suggests, "If [Mrs.] Vogler's silence queries art, art returns the question, measuring the value and consequences of an actress's refusal to continue. Vogler, then, is not the voice of *Persona*; rather, the film gives voice to her silence" (Bergman 181). In film after film from his mature period—one thinks of the hillside picnic in *The Seventh Seal* (1957), the deus ex machina ending of *The Magician*, and the three sisters in a swing on a warm autumn day at the conclusion of *Cries and Whispers*—Bergman reminds us of the illusory element in all moments of clarity, community, peace, and happiness, and then confirms that the meaning contained in these images is something more than merely a sentimental religious faith or an existential joke. By such illusions, he seems to say, do we all manage to live.

As much as any other work in the history of cinema, *Persona* draws attention to the illusion that is film and the phantom that is character. In its entropic winding down, both protagonists tentatively resume their designated roles: Elisabet is seen in costume; Alma is seen in uniform. Having exposed the nurse's idealist self-conception of a life devoted to healing the sick, the actress's existentialist experiment in self-creation, and the doctor's psychiatric model of self-therapy, the film restores the characters to their former roles—but not to their former isolated and complacent selves. "I've learned a lot," Alma remarks bitterly toward the end. The attentive spectator of *Persona* will have learned as well, about the necessary illusion from which all human identity, as well as all art, is constructed.

CHAPTER THREE

❖

Incarnations of the Confidence Man

The movement itself is the only truth.

—*The Magician*

Among the vast array of readily recognizable character types within the history of the cinema—including not only the Westerner and the gangster (Robert Warshow), the virgin and the vamp (Sumiko Higashi), but also such "complex" figures as the prostitute-with-heart-of-gold and clown-with-breaking-heart—this book concentrates on the phantom, an enigmatic but nonetheless definable type. The introductory chapter suggested numerous permutations of this figure; the chapter on *Persona* analyzed the reflexive function of the master trope's incarnation as a double. The habit of perceiving represented persons typologically, of course, applies to life as well as film reception and remains inevitably reductive whenever "glimpses of behavior—brief vignettes—are taken to be touchstones of larger being" (Hochman 70). For this reason as well as practical considerations of the book's length, I am not primarily concerned here with trying to produce a taxonomy of character types under the general category of "Phantoms of the Cinema." But I am arguing for a connection between the elusive nature of a certain kind of character haunting many of the most compelling modern films and the status of cinema itself as, in Raymond Bellour's phrase, an "unattainable text" among its sister arts. Bellour has in mind not simply the relative inaccessibility (until very recently with the commercial distribution of video facsimiles) of the motion picture as a material object but rather the "unquotable" nature of the film text, which "on the one hand . . . spreads in space like a picture; on the other . . . plunges into time, like a story" (25) and which, as Metz has demonstrated, consists of no less than five modes of expression (phonetic sound, written titles, musical sound, noises, plus the moving photographic image).

The relation between character as unknowable and cinema as imaginary signifier/unattainable text carries both psychological and historical implications: it paradoxically deepens our attraction to a fugitive, untrustworthy image, and it confirms our present-day immersion in a world of perpetual images, a simulacrum.[12] The reflexive aspect of the phantom character becomes more apparent when the protagonist, rather than being simply a site of mystery as in Joseph Cotten's Uncle Charlie (*Shadow of a Doubt*, 1943) or Cary Grant's Johnnie (*Suspicion*, 1941), takes the form of an artist, as in several of Bergman's films following *Persona* (*Hour of the Wolf* [1968], *Shame* [1968], *Autumn Sonata* [1978]), or, as in the texts presently under discussion, a confidence man. Both artist and con man have a long history in literary fiction, the confidence man often serving as the author's alter ego, reminding the reader of her desire to be deceived in order to be entertained and warning the writer of the excesses of his art.

Although his origins can be traced at least as far back as Chaucer's Pardoner, the confidence man in literature has generally been regarded as a modern character type, a development of the primitive trickster reflecting and ultimately subverting the growing diversity, literacy, and self-assurance of an emergent urban culture. His evolution, in this regard, rather neatly parallels the development of the movies during the twentieth century. Certainly, Georges Méliès may stand as cinema's first great confidence man, both as an actor transforming his own image on the screen and as a director exploiting his audience's naive faith in the objective transcription of reality signified by that image. While an affinity with the confidence man has stirred the imagination of many writers, including Melville, Twain, Nathanael West, Mann, Nabokov, and Fowles, filmmakers following in the expressionist tradition of Méliès may have sensed this identification even more strongly. As we have seen, Bergman delighted in the deceptions of "the conjurer's art":

I have worked it out that if I see a film which has a running time of one hour, I sit through twenty-seven minutes of complete darkness—the blankness between frames. When I show a film I am guilty of deceit, I use an apparatus which is constructed to take advantage of a certain human weakness, an apparatus with which I can sway my audience in a highly emotional manner—make them laugh, scream with fright, smile, believe in fairy stories, become indignant, feel shocked, charmed, deeply moved or perhaps even yawn with boredom. Thus I am either an imposter or, *when the audience is willing to be taken in*, a conjurer. (Four Screenplays 15; italics mine)

In the last sentence, the director expands his initial understanding of film art to include psychological as well as physiological processes. By encompassing the spectator's complicity in the game along with the projector's capacity to enhance the artist's deceptions, Bergman's depiction of filmmaking as a confidence game restores the word "willing" to Coleridge's famous description of the audience's suspension of disbelief in the artifice of representation. It is a restoration crucial to the conception of character as a represented person that I have proposed as an alternative to the structuralist/semiotic model.

Beyond the ocular deceptions of flicker fusion and persistence of vision that create the illusion of movement, beyond the ideological effects of the cinematic apparatus (as defined by Baudry), film narrative depends on the audience's temporary confidence in the presence of projected images that remain inherently deceptive. The spectator cooperates with the filmmaker in ignoring the fact that the recorded objects and actors are not really there: when they were, during shooting, the audience was absent; when the audience is present, during screening, they remain absent. This truism (perhaps uninteresting in itself) helps to explain the enduring appeal of the confidence man in film, even in relatively banal texts like *Elmer Gantry* (1960) or *A Face in the Crowd* (1957): he is both a cipher, his identity "absorbed into the illusions he creates for those around him" (Blair 24) and, as Braudy has suggested, a double for the cinema's process of signification, implying that "character itself, so palpably before you, is merely a construction" (24). Melville made much the same point throughout his novel *The Confidence Man*, anticipating by more than a century the structuralists' argument about character being merely an agency of plot but also relating the chameleon qualities of his protagonist to the ambiguity underlying all human identity: "Nobody knows who anybody is. The data which life furnishes, toward forming a true estimate of any being, are as insufficient to that end as in geometry one side given would be to determine the triangle" (209).

At the same time he subverts all efforts to know him, the confidence man displays a virtuosity that makes him seem more than "merely a construction." As the double of the artist, he may be admired for his "technical facility" as well as "some larger promise derived from his power to inspire belief' (Lindberg 7). His moral character in the application of his talent, like his origins, personal relationships, and private experiences, remains fundamentally uncertain. By exploiting "a certain weakness" in his victims, the con man as artist figure exposes what Nathanael West once called the "natural antipathy" (25) between the performer and the audience, an imperfectly repressed antagonism built on mutual need. The confidence game in the movie theater, in its play of willing suspension of disbelief, reveals both the artist's urge to exhibit and the spectator's compulsion to look—and in looking, to believe. While the transaction seems naturally to favor the con artist's superior knowledge ("Grifter's got an irresistible urge to be wise"— *The Grifters* [1990]), the performance depends on bravado as much as genius (Hooker: "He's not as tough as he looks." Gondorff: "Neither are we."—*The Sting* [1973]). The result may prove triumphant for the hustler and therapeutic for the mark only so long as the game holds them both in the dark. When the credits crawl and the theater lights return, the character on screen whose beguiling presence deceived and disturbed us recedes to Metz's "primordial *elsewhere*," while we in the audience are restored to the quotidian.

The basic structure of the con man's modus operandi has remained relatively constant since Robert Greene first described it in *A Notable Discovery of Cozenage* (1591):

> The con man and his confederates seek out a well-to-do prospect in a context permitting easy contact with strangers. They establish friendly relations as a means to arousing his curiosity about a money-making scheme, the more sure because it is dishonest. They arrange a "convincer," a trial case where the victim reaps large profits from risking a small amount. If they play their cards right, the victim will eagerly insist on being allowed to join in on the largest scale he can afford. Inevitably some "mischance" occurs between the time when he turns his money over to the con man and the time

when the rewards were to have been reaped. The victim is abandoned, stripped of his cash and also any moral basis for complaining to the police. (Blair 20)

Today, this method of "cozenage" goes by the name of "short con," a scam that exploits ordinary human weakness and deprives the victim of cash and cause for complaint. The "long con," on the other hand, requires sustained virtuosity and exacts a more profound price. Transcending his "technical facility" to craft merely sensory illusions, the long con artist—something like Mephistopheles in the Faust story—creates a world where illusion and reality become indistinguishable and robs the mark of not just money but a system of belief.

All representational arts, as Plato and Coleridge understood, play a short con in order to function: the artist fabricates an illusion that the audience temporarily accepts as truth. Classical film, as we have noted, has usually followed the path of least resistance and profited from the viewer's faith that the camera does not lie. "The cinema, despite its superficial modernity and technological razzle-dazzle, has generally fostered a retrograde illusionistic aesthetic" (Stam 10). Most movies about con men—*The Sting* and *The Grifters* will be my examples here—do the same, thereby distancing their audiences somewhat from the dupes on screen while encouraging identification with the sharpsters. These works ultimately flatter as well as entertain their patrons by foregrounding the "game" without exploring the implications of "confidence."[13]

On the other hand, the past century (more precisely, texts produced after 1914 belonging to the modern period) has seen a significant counter-realist body of works that reflexively underscore their own status as illusions. These texts—Gide's fiction, Magritte's paintings, Brecht's plays—execute a kind of long con, claiming an authenticity for themselves in a world of pervasive deception by openly declaring their falseness in order to verify, paradoxically, their truth. Thus, a literary tradition dating back at least as far as Renaissance dramas like *The Knight of the Burning Pestle* and eighteenth-century novels like *Joseph Andrews* and *Tristram Shandy* has adopted various disruptive strategies designed to test the limits of the audience's confidence, manifested by their continuance of the fictional game. In contrast to George Roy Hill's *The Sting* and Stephen Frears's *The Grifters*, movies that successfully entertained mass audiences by providing solvable problems, suspense, and surprise while observing the conventions of verisimilitude, Bergman's

The Magician and David Mamet's *House of Games* (1987) move in the direction of modernist and (in Mamet's case) postmodernist narrative by foregrounding the counterfeit existence of their protagonists (beyond their duplicitous trade) and the artificiality of key images to suggest a "larger promise" beyond material proof. As they call into question what normally passes for diegetic reality, these two films preserve the phantom character of the confidence man, reaffirming in a self-conscious way the elusive aura of the very process of cinematic signification.

SHORT CON: *THE STING* AND *THE GRIFTERS*

The most commercially successful of all modern films about the confidence man, *The Sting* introduces its paradigmatic plot through old-fashioned intertitles that link the historical diegesis (Chicago during Prohibition) with the cinematic sign: "The Set-Up," "The Hook," "The Tale," "The Wire," "The Shut-Out," "The Sting." This narrative structure closely coincides with Robert Greene's sixteenth-century description of "cozenage" but raises the stakes by extending the set-up. Two grifters, Henry Gondorff (Paul Newman) and Johnny Hooker (Robert Redford), cheat a big-time criminal at cards as a way of setting him up for a much bigger loss in an off-track betting scam. Although the diegesis presents an elaborate long con scheme, the movie itself plays only a traditional Hollywood short con with its audience. The plot, segmented by the intertitles, is not only formulaic but signalled in advance; with the exception of a climactic flourish (the shammed death of Gondorff, quickly revealed), the spectator remains a privileged insider who recognizes the clever illusions designed to trick the villainous gangster and thus remains superior to him. Moreover, the two confidence men can be immediately identified as America's leading movie stars of the day—Newman and Redford—reprising their immensely popular roles as wise-cracking heroes in Hill's earlier hit, *Butch Cassidy and the Sundance Kid* (1969). The viewer need only accept their identities as Gandorff and Hooker for the duration of this particular picture, while within the diegesis they are readily understood as stereotypes of the old pro and (as Hooker is frequently called) the "Kid." Charming, clever, and handsome, they are "characters" in quotation marks, overdetermined by a small cluster of traits and limited to their agency in the complicated plot.

In one anomalous sequence, however, *The Sting* does employ the specific technical facility available in the cinema to con the spectator. Midway through the movie, Hooker is chased down a dead-end tenement alley by the villain Lonigan's thugs, whereupon he seems to disappear into thin air. Only after the would-be assassins search the narrow brick-walled space and leave the frame does the camera track back to reveal a previously unseen manhole, which is held in close-up until the scene changes. Hooker never peeps out, though the camera movement has resolved the mystery of his phantom-like evanescence. In this single moment of (probably unintentional) reflexivity, the movie confirms the presence of absence that characterizes both the cinema's imaginary signifier and the confidence man's particular way of operating.

Like *The Sting*, *The Grifters* is reflexive primarily in regard to style, paying homage to the urban landscapes and low-key lighting of film noir just as the earlier movie employed intertitles, swish pans, and soundstage sets to evoke (imprecisely) the bygone studio era. Despite its initial presentation of the three protagonists concealed behind dark glasses in a split screen composition, the grifters of the title—two of them women—are characterized only slightly less schematically than the stereotypes that populate *The Sting*. Aside from their clear roles in an Oedipal configuration (offering critics ample opportunity to elaborate psychoanalytic readings of the text), they represent three distinctive kinds of con men. Roy Dillon (John Cusack), by his own definition, is "strictly short con," motivated by profit alone. His girlfriend, Myra Langtry (Annette Bening), dreams of the long con, inspired by a mixture of adventuresomeness and compulsion. Roy's mother, Lily (Angelica Huston), survives them both by being stronger than Roy and more clever than Myra while remaining a behind-the-scenes operator. Each character has a certain attractiveness—Roy's vulnerability, Myra's sexiness, Lily's professionalism—but none personifies the elusive quality of the cinematic sign. If not quite as transparent as the caricatures in *The Sting*, neither are they sites of unknowable character like Melville's portrait of the confidence man. The evocative aspect of *The Grifters* derives more from its homage to genre (even the automobiles are all large, suggesting an earlier era) and its nods to Freud and feminism than from its conjuring of phantoms. While these two movies create much of their appeal by foregrounding the deceptive game that cinema always plays with the spectator, the pair of films that follow in this discussion double the stakes by testing the audience's faith not merely in the honesty of a particular character, but in the efficacy of conceiving a notion of character itself.

LONG CON: *THE MAGICIAN*

Working apart from the genre conventions, star system, and commercial considerations of the Hollywood studio system, Bergman created a succession of films that meditate upon various issues of art: the moral responsibilities of the artist, the ambivalent relationship between the performer and the audience, the problematic quality of any art's attempt to represent reality. Among such works as *Sawdust and Tinsel* (1953), *The Seventh Seal, Hour of the Wolf, Shame,* and *Fanny and Alexander* (1982), *Persona,* as we have seen, remains the most self-conscious about the specific medium of film. *The Magician,* however, stands as the most incisive study of the artist as confidence man. In contrast to the later American depictions of the con artist, Bergman's Albert Emanuel Vogler projects a variety of allegorical identities—Christ symbol, artist figure, existentialist antihero, alter ego—yet endures as an enigmatic figure not only to the diegetic characters but to the audience in the theater as well. "Who *are* you?" one character asks him early in the film, a question repeated by another at the end, each time without a reply.[14]

In contrast to *The Sting* and *The Grifters,* the plot of *The Magician* is quite simple: in nineteenth-century Sweden, a touring troupe of small-time mountebanks calling themselves "Vogler's Magnetic Health Theater" must spend the night at Consul Egerman's (Erland Josephson) home, where their leader (Max von Sydow) submits to a demeaning inquiry from the royal physician, Dr. Vergérus (Gunnar Bjornstrand), and the chief of police, Starbeck (Tovio Pawlo), in hopes of obtaining a permit. After being mocked and exposed as an apparent charlatan, Vogler avenges himself with a powerful, partially inexplicable conjuring act. Humiliated and cast off despite the impact he has had, Vogler is saved by a last second deus ex machina (one that disturbed many of the film's critics), an unexpected summons from the king to give a performance in Stockholm. Bergman's resolution of the narrative completes a long con perpetrated on the audience rather than the diegetic characters, all of whom accept the royal decree as genuine. That the document is dated 14 July—Bergman's birthday—only confirms that *he,* and not Vogler, is the film's ultimate magician.

The structure of *The Magician* involves a succession of "short cons"—obvious tricks that function only temporarily and depend entirely on the spectator's suppression of doubt—designed to set up the miraculous (or preposterous) ending. As Vogler's wife (Ingrid Thulin) initially describes their magic lantern to the officials as "an absurd and harmless toy," Bergman disarms the attentive spectator by announcing the transparent unreality of the film's initial images.[15] For example, the first close-ups of Vogler's face (the film's Swedish title is the word for "face," *ansiktet*) reveal that he is disguised by a false beard and wig—in short, *masked*, a perception soon confirmed by the dying actor Spegel (Bengt Ekerot), who immediately sees through the magician's make-up and asks if he is an actor too (fig. 11). Many persons in the film audience may also unmask Vogler at first sight but unconsciously repress recognition of the disguise (knowing that all actors are in some sense disguised) in order to avoid acknowledging the director's failure to perfect his illusion—particularly a director as accomplished as Bergman. Because they have not yet seen Vogler "out of character," the audience knows nothing of the protagonist's self beyond the role he has assumed. To compound the facile deception, the magician's wife is dressed as a man—and answers to the name "Aman"—though she is obviously otherwise. Thus, the film begins to build the spectators' confidence in their own inside knowledge of the fabricated illusion, while at the same time it induces their collaboration in preserving that illusion.

Spegel's "death" in the opening sequence provides further illustration of the short con Bergman is playing. The actor's performance is patently theatrical: after being seized by violent tremors, he seems to collapse, then histrionically describes the progress of death through his body before apparently expiring at the very point of defining death. As with the Voglers' masquerades, the spectator assumes, despite the unreality of the exhibition, that Spegel has, in fact, breathed his last, albeit hammily. Later in the film, however, this scene's status as a set-up becomes apparent when Spegel reappears and gives a much more credible performance of the same action: "I have become convincing as a ghost," he tells Vogler, "which I never was as an actor." *This* Spegel reverberates with a double identity. "As an actor," he is merely a diegetic character, quite literally an agent of the plot (his body will be substituted for Vogler's in the subsequent simulation of the magician's death); "as a ghost," however, he stands for the cinematic sign, which renders an illusion of presence despite the actual absence of the referent

FIGURE 11. *The Magician*

and thus represents all characters as phantoms of their own fictional selves. The film "apparatus," as we have been insisting, leaves only a trace of the actor's presence before the camera. Thus, when Spegel describes himself as "a shadow of a shadow," he defines his appearance as a film actor rather than an actor on stage.[16] His dying words now confirm the reflexive function of this farewell performance: "The movement itself is the only truth." By making Spegel's second death scene so intensely disturbing in contrast to the false emotions conjured by the first, Bergman demonstrates the force of the "long con" his film has constructed. The spectator is encouraged to believe that here the actor has "really" died—despite having been fooled by the same act before and despite knowing at a subconscious level that the actor Bengt Ekerot (who had previously played the role of Death in Bergman's *The Seventh Seal*) has not really died—just as the viewer will be inclined to accept the film's contrived happy ending.

Spegel's death is followed the next morning by Vogler's performance for the bourgeois gathering in Egerman's drawing room. From this point on, the film consistently positions the spectator as the filmmaker's mark, just as the skeptical officials are manipulated by the magician. Vogler's in-house exhibition parallels the structure of Bergman's film: an initial display of obvious illusion gives way to increasingly frightening, inexplicable tricks. The performance begins with a crude levitation that Starbeck abruptly ruins by drawing back the screen behind which an assistant manipulates the pulleys and ropes holding Aman aloft. Despite this abject failure, the audience giggles in delight and Tubal, the troupe's impresario, continues as if nothing has gone awry. Having previously acknowledged the mechanical nature of their deceptions ("A game, nothing else. We use various kinds of apparatus, mirrors, and projectors") and then been exposed in mid-act, Vogler's performers are prepared to exploit their patrons' confidence. Tubal invites the police chief's wife to step forward, whereupon, under Vogler's hypnotic spell, she insults Starbeck's gross appearance and manners, then returns to her husband and friends with no memory of what she has revealed. For a climax, Vogler performs "The Invisible Chains," reducing the powerful servant Antonsson to a helpless slave of the magician's "spiritual power." Once the spell is finally broken, when the clock strikes the hour, the servant exacts his revenge by savagely seizing Vogler and strangling him, although this sudden death, like Spegel's first scene, requires considerable credulity from the spectator since Vogler expires in a matter of seconds. Thus, the public performance, in which the magician exhibited genuine power over his initially distrustful audience, ends in apparent disaster. But this demonstration proves to be merely a rehearsal—another set-up—for Vogler's private encore that provides the climax to *The Magician*.

After locking himself in the attic with Vergérus, who has been intent on performing an autopsy on the magician's (actually Spegel's) body, Vogler, now unmasked, acts out his repressed hostility against the audience ("I hate them," he has told his wife when they were alone) by terrorizing the doctor with a succession of macabre sensations. Bergman reaffirms the reflexive nature of this sequence in two ways: first, through a series of images referring to distorted vision—an eyeball in an inkstand, reflections in a smoky mirror, Vergérus's shattered spectacles—and second, through several cinematic devices that intensify the gothic effect. As Vogler stalks the half-blind doctor who crawls backwards in fear, the director for the first time fully draws upon the arsenal of film's technical resources: tracking shots, acute camera angles, non-diegetic sound, low-key, spot lighting. Perhaps most terrifying is the unfamiliar, undisguised image of Vogler's face, his natural features so disturbing precisely because he is "out of character," the artist as sycophant transformed into dark avenger.

His tour de force finally broken by Vergérus's involuntary scream and subsequent release, Vogler must revert to humiliating dependency, confessing his "cheap trick" and begging Vergérus for money, then going unrecognized by Mrs. Egerman, who had worshipped him the night before. Looking at the magician's pathetic figure, the film spectator may readily forget the powerful experience he has just created and agree with the restored Vergérus, who pronounces him a total fraud. Only then does Bergman intervene with the plot device that abruptly saves Vogler's company. While many commentators have noted how the royal request represents the director's own trick to redeem his artist figure from the critics, few if any have examined the visual and aural dimensions of this ultimate display.[17] With the arrival of the royal coach, the weather instantly changes (via a straight cut) from pouring rain to brilliant sunshine—with no puddles in the street to preserve even a semblance of mimetic continuity. Non-diegetic march music accompanies the magician's triumphant reprieve and the troupe's departure in the closing long shot. Here Bergman flaunts his movie magic with a final bit of bravura: after the coach disappears up the cobbled street and the brassy march music concludes, leaving behind only the rattle of a swinging street lantern, the band music unexpectedly resumes for a brief encore. The spectator has been fooled one last time—if only for a few seconds—by the false ending.

The melodramatic display of Vogler's power in the attic and the comic resolution imposed by Bergman illustrate something beyond the mere "technical facility" of the confidence man. They confirm as well an authentic "higher promise" distinguishing the artist from the craftsman and redeeming the deceptions of his confidence game. Vogler's effect at times transcends the trivial consequences of mesmerism, as when, for example, the grieving Mrs. Egerman kisses his hand and sees there a stigmata not evident to the audience. "You will explain why my child died, what God meant," she tells him. "That's why you have come." Although he conveys no such message, he does bring about the reconciliation of Mrs. Egerman and her husband. Certainly his control over Antonsson defies rational explanation, as does his manipulation of objects in the attic. Vogler mutely acknowledges his hidden gifts during the initial interrogation when Vergérus asks if he can induce visions and later when he confides to his wife his fears of losing his spiritual powers. By announcing at the very beginning that all is illusion—Vogler wears a disguise, Spegel shams his own death, Aman is a woman—the film enlightens the spectator in order to prepare an ultimate demonstration of its own capacity to mystify. Even Vogler's fate, after all, remains undetermined: the very artificiality of the ending leaves the outcome of the royal performance uncertain. Modifying the more conventional narrative method of *The Seventh Seal* made two years earlier, *The Magician* deliberately deploys allegory to subvert the allegorical mode of interpretation, insisting instead that "the movement itself is the only truth." Although that movement in the cinema may be only an illusion, it is, as we have suggested earlier, a *necessary* illusion. Thus, Vogler's exit line, so reminiscent of Bergman's description of the tools of his trade, echoes his creator's pride: "Pack my apparatus . . . but be careful. It is very valuable."

LONG CON: *HOUSE OF GAMES*

Nearly thirty years after the release of *The Magician* (nearly a century and a half later in diegetic time), Mamet's *House of Games* reasserts the cinema's power to deceive and mystify but promises no redeeming payoff from the confidence game. In the postmodern world implied by the title, conning is simply what everyone—grifters, psychiatrists, authors, filmmakers—does for a living. In its formal strategies, however, *House of Games* shares with *The Magician* a reflexive gamesmanship that plays with the spectator's voyeurism and credulity to pull off a long con leaving the audience rather than the fictional characters mystified and betrayed. Unlike *The Sting* and *The Grifters*, these two films go beyond transient surprises or thrills to inform viewers of the duplicitous, seductive ontology of the cinema, thereby complicating the audience's sense of moral or intellectual superiority to the con man and his marks since their complicity in the movie theater remains a precondition to being deceived.

The plot of *House of Games* involves an elaborate scheme whereby a professional con man known only as "Mike" (Joe Mantegna) manipulates a successful psychiatrist and best-selling author, Dr. Margaret Ford (Lindsay Crouse). After discovering that she has been seduced, robbed, and abandoned, Margaret tracks down Mike in an airport and kills him when, at gunpoint, he refuses to beg for his life. The denouement then strongly suggests that Margaret has gotten away with murder. Most critical discussion of *House of Games* has focussed on this problematic ending—a melodramatic inversion of *The Magician*'s comic rescue—without adequately acknowledging how the film's entire narrative design underscores the inherent unreality of the fiction through misdirection, stylization, and illogical discourse among the characters. Mamet employs these earlier set-ups to convince his audience to accept (or at least rationalize) a patently false resolution, leading even sophisticated viewers like William Van Wert clutching at Lacanian models to "explain" the psychotherapeutic function of the final two scenes. While Van Wert quite perceptively notes "how much the con men depend on Margaret's voyeurism for the success of the various cons" and how Mamet uses the camera as a "co-conspirator" in their operation (5), he subordinates the reflexive function of such "tells" in favor of a naturalistic interpretation—basically, that the ending is all Margaret's fantasy projected to effect her own "therapeutic purge"—of what remains, despite his efforts at explication, an adamantly stylized fiction. What Van Wert calls the "master con" refers only to the elaborate scam of Mike and his cronies to fleece Margaret; in so doing, he lapses into treating the characters as if they were real, with extensive personal histories and fully developed motivations, and so becomes himself the unwitting mark of Mamet's own master con. In fact, Mike has no individual background (his claim to having once been a Marine, for example, being a "bit" in a short con), no intimate secrets to reveal; Margaret is similarly lacking in a verifiable personal past but is known only by her professional life as revealed in the journal she meticulously compiles.

The film's unusual opening shot employs calculated misdirection to disorient the uninitiated spectator and then to secure conventional trust. The camera first records an unidentifiable textured mass, then begins a horizontal track left until the image can be recognized as a stone and concrete wall. The tracking shot continues, apparently to follow a woman in a white dress walking in the same direction across a plaza, until it reveals a woman in red in the foreground who seems to be looking at her. In fact, the object of the camera's and the second woman's attention turns out to be Margaret Ford, who has been standing in the distance all along. As in the con man's set-up or the magician's sleight of hand, Mamet has initially used the moving camera to deceive, then lets the viewer in on the trick to re-establish faith that the camera does not lie.

In a similar sort of set-up, the physical setting for *House of Games*, both the unspecified city in which Dr. Ford practices psychiatry and the address at 211 Beaumont Street where Mike conducts his business, suggests the imaginary realm in which the cinema constructs its own particular illusions and the postmodernist conception of the simulacrum comprised of empty signifiers. Unlike the specific locales of *The Sting* ("Joliet, Illinois/September 1936," as announced in a title card) and *The Grifters* (Los Angeles, with sequences in Texas and Phoenix), the urban landscape for *House of Games* remains indeterminate,[18] evoking both the inaccessible "primordial *elsewhere*" that Metz has defined as the place signified by all cinema and the triumph of sheer spectacle that Baudrillard identifies with postmodernism.

The establishing shot that situates the "House of Games" reinforces the theatricality of the playwright Mamet's film-directing debut at the same time it subtly signifies how *all* places viewed in the movies are intrinsically less real (because not really present) than even the most artificial of stage sets. Accompanied by soft, jazzy xylophone music, a carefully composed long shot frames the pool hall across a dimly lit, rain-slicked, and totally empty street. A steady cloud of steam emanates from a manhole, enhancing the stylized mood; the camera remains fixed instead of tracking Margaret as she crosses the street. The same scene, complete with synchronized steam, repeats when Margaret revisits this place that looks like the flip side of Sesame Street, as familiar as it is unreal (fig. 12).

The schematic design underlying the presentation of Beaumont Street extends to the film's narrative structure, dialogue, and performances. The structural formality is indicated by the opening and closing scenes in which Margaret, wearing sunglasses, responds to requests from strangers to autograph her book and by the various set pieces—short cons at the card table, on the street, in the Western Union office—that inspire both Margaret's and the audience's trust. As Billy Hahn, one of Dr. Ford's patients who is also involved in Mike's scam, tells her, "the whole thing is a con game." This perception, of course, applies to the film as a whole, as Mamet further indicates through his characters' stilted dialogue and mannered behavior: Margaret, on first meeting Mike, says, "Talk turkey, pal"; the poker players, like a postmodernist chorus, converse entirely in the ritual argot of their trade, commenting on a high-stakes poker game, "It happens to the best, it happens to the rest," "A man with style is a man who can smile." With the exception of Margaret's brief conversations with her mentor Maria, everything in *House of Games* seems over-rehearsed.

The card game in which the con men's attempt to trick Margaret out of six thousand dollars seems foiled when she notices that the gambler's pistol is actually a leaking squirt gun later proves to be a set-up for the master con, Mike's and also Mamet's. It works in precisely the same way as Vogler's aborted levitation routine. Once exposed, the con men offer no apology; after all, they have not presented themselves as entirely trustworthy in the first place. Once Margaret believes that she has seen through the illusion (just in time to save her money), she assumes that the game is now over and that everything to follow will either include her as an "insider" or else be the real thing. Her choice, then, is to become a collaborator or a fool. In the immediate aftermath of the "crumbed play" in the House of Games, Margaret is both: she eagerly becomes Mike's pupil as he instructs her in the tricks of his trade; yet at the end of the evening she asks him to return Billy Hahn's IOU by appealing to his personal honesty ("Are you a man of your word?" she naively asks). His compliance ("What's right is right") seals her trust.

Mamet concludes this long sequence with a set piece of magic played only for the film spectator. After Margaret drives off in a cab, Mike remains spotlighted and alone in the middle of Beaumont Street. Silhouetted by back lighting, he flips a coin from one hand

FIGURE 12. *House of Games*

to the other, then makes the coin disappear (fig. 13). Here, in a single, formal shot without any diegetic function, Mamet inscribes the paradigm of presence of absence and links it to both the cinematic sign and the ephemerality of character. Like Vogler, Mike can create some inexplicable illusions. Like Bergman, Mamet has held some surprises in reserve. All that Margaret and the film audience have seen so far, as one of the veteran hustlers puts it, is but "a little page in the history of the short con."

Mike's master con, which involves the same kind of inevitable "mischance" in a financial transaction that Greene described in his *Cozenage*, succeeds in extracting from Margaret an eighty-thousand-dollar payoff, but like any film once run through the projector, it cannot indefinitely sustain the illusion. Without his confederates, without his "apparatus" (blank bullets, fake blood, false uniforms, artfully arranged hotel rooms), the confidence man must rely on sheer bravado to appease his vengeful victim. In *The Magician*, Vogler, stripped of all resources and lacking faith in his own powers, grovels in a vain effort to solicit his audience's pity in order to survive. Mike, on the other hand, refuses to beg when confronted by Margaret and instead calls her bluff. In a climax that recalls the ending to West's *Miss Lonelyhearts*—a novel in which characters are also two-dimensional and speak at each other in rhetorical dialogue filled with clichés, and where another con man is ultimately shot by a disciple whom he has betrayed—Mike miscalculates the disillusion his deception has provoked and, unable to escape the role he has created, dies "in character."

While the con game conceived in the House of Games has been exposed as an imposture, *House of Games* continues to conjure up its own version of the long con, reaffirming the postmodern perspective Billy Hahn articulated at the outset in accusing Margaret ("It's all a con game"). Neither Mike's crime nor Margaret's "cure" possesses any reality, any meaning, beyond the desire of Mamet's audience to trust what they see. Like the ending of *The Magician*, the film's final two scenes call the *spectator's* bluff, asking her to accept on faith, first, a deserted airport at 9:45 P.M. with an unlocked baggage conveyor area; second, a fatal shooting in which six rounds are fired at point blank range without a single sign of blood; and third, a noted psychiatrist who commits cold-blooded murder without emotional or legal consequences. The airport resembles a displaced House of Games: a generic, depopulated environment whose supposedly forbidden baggage loading area parallels

FIGURE 13. *House of Games*

the back room in which the exchange of high stakes bluffing occurs. Margaret's pistol similarly recalls both the squirt gun that gave away the short con and the revolver loaded with blanks that clinched the master con. The film has already openly proclaimed and then illustrated how everything is an illusion ("I'm a con man," Mike tells Margaret early on, "You don't have to delude yourself"); now it demonstrates just how much the movie goer desires to be deluded.

The denouement confounds any attempt to understand the fundamental mystery of character that the confidence man personifies—and that psychiatry implicitly denies. Like the reprieved Vogler, Margaret is "reborn" in this scene, but as a figure no less mysterious than Mike, her true mentor: tanned from a recent vacation (she had been a workaholic), dressed in a bright floral print (she had favored monochromatic tailored suits), free from guilt (she had agonized over her patients), she joins Maria for lunch in a fashionable restaurant. In the world the film has created in which being is synonymous with role-playing, she has discovered her own character as a confidence man (she had previously repeated Billy Hahn's accusation about her profession to Maria) and, in these final moments, has become comfortable with the role. In the airport, she had successfully called Mike's bluff; now she misdirects a stranger's attention and steals her lighter, smiling with pleasure at her triumph. As the film's ultimate con man, Mamet ends *House of Games* with this suggestive subterfuge, evoking the last sentence of Melville's novel: "Something further may follow of this Masquerade."

CHAPTER FOUR

◈

Reviving the Undead:
Herzog's Remake of Nosferatu

When Georges Méliès's camera jammed on that famous, probably apocryphal afternoon at the Place de l'Opéra and the bus he had been shooting was transformed into a hearse during projection, he apprehended for perhaps the first time the ghostly quality of the cinema's particular mode of representation. That phantom image of the hearse, I have been suggesting, has proven to be an evocative symbol of film's unique process of simultaneously deceiving and enthralling the spectator by substituting an illusory presence for an absent referent, rendering as "undead" a departed object by animating projected shadows and light, often revealing the disturbing contours of familiar shapes. Filmmakers and audiences ever since have been attracted to the depiction of spirits and monsters that not only seem to express certain imperfectly repressed human desires but that also may reflect something about the idiosyncratic signifying system of the cinema itself. Certainly Mary Shelley's monster, Robert Louis Stevenson's Mr. Hyde, and Bram Stoker's Count Dracula today seem rather long-winded intellectuals compared to their original movie incarnations. Is it because as the offspring of uncontrollable technology, doubles of unstable wills, or fleeting creatures of darkness, these celluloid characters exhibit something uncanny and threatening inherent in the very experience of watching films?

Among the gallery of screen monsters, the vampire seems especially well suited to portray both the parasitical quality of the film artist's exploitation of the audience (as in *Persona*) and the elusive, insubstantial nature of the film image. Unlike the grotesque, omnipotent, oversized creatures of most horror movies, the vampire remains a *phantom*—a vision of uncertain substance—rather than a certifiable *monster*. All such demonic or freakish embodiments of horror have been regarded as doubles either of repressed desires (violence in Hyde, lust in Dracula) or fears (pregnancy in the Frankenstein monster, puberty in the Wolf Man), but the vampire alone seems the perfect phantom double of the cinematic apparatus, a "simulation machine," as Baudry has put it, offering "perceptions which are really representations." The vampire frightens us with its shadow rather than its substance, in Benjamin's terms the "aura" of a mechanically produced work of art. Being neither suddenly alive nor larger-than-life but rather "undead," it evokes not merely revulsion at the material but longing for the mystical. As a paradigmatic figure of the cinema, especially in Murnau's *Nosferatu, a Symphony of Horror* (*Nosferatu, eine Symphonie des Grauens*, 1922) and Herzog's remake, *Nosferatu, the Vampyre* (*Nosferatu, Phantom der Nacht*, 1979), the vampire on film represents the imaginary so effectively because it *is* the imaginary (Metz, Imaginary 44).

In addition to these German versions of the vampire myth, there have been innumerable American and British adaptations, the most noteworthy of which include Tod Browning's *Dracula* (1931), Terence Fisher's *Horror of Dracula* (1958), John Badham's *Dracula* (1978), and Francis Coppola's *Bram Stoker's Dracula* (1992), not to mention dozens of sequels, spinoffs, and parodies. Each of the six major retellings to date, starring Max Schreck, Klaus Kinski, Bela Lugosi, Christopher Lee, Frank Langella, and Gary Oldham in the title role, has sufficiently revitalized the power of the original novel to refute Alain Resnais's oft-cited rejection of adaptations as merely "warmed-over meals." Murnau's and Herzog's *Nosferatus*, however, remain more resonant and compelling than the other Dracula movies for two related reasons: first, they present the Count as a complex, even sympathetic protagonist rather than the evil monster of Stoker's novel; second, they suggest a profound relation between this indefinable characterization and the phantom images projected by the cinematic apparatus. Their modernity, in short, derives from both their inherent ambiguity and a certain reflexiveness missing in the other versions.[19] Unlike their English-speaking counterparts, Schreck and Kinski manage to signify elusiveness rather than presence, lack rather than excess, entropy rather than energy. Their Draculas are less the doubles of perverse creative energy (the "love that never dies," as the advertisement for Coppola's version would have it) than the phantoms of the cinema itself.

Each of these six movies (unlike, say, *Abbot and Costello Meet Frankenstein* [in which Lugosi appears prominently as Dracula] or *Buffy the Vampire Killer*) generally present themselves as adaptations—"doubles" or "copies" of a literary text, Stoker's novel, in a new discursive mode, film. Because it follows so closely the visual design of Murnau's original—essentially copying the costuming, make-up, plot structure, and performance style, borrowing some of the dialogue ("What a beautiful throat your wife has!") and camera angles, even shooting the very same buildings in Lubeck that Murnau had employed—Herzog's *Nosferatu* may be more precisely defined as an homage, the remake of a cinematic text rather than a literary classic "whose purpose is to pay tribute to an earlier film rather than usurp its place of honor" (Leitch 144). Despite the director's claim that, "We are not remaking *Nosferatu*, but bringing it to new life and new character for a new age" (Andrews 33), his film, unlike the others, cannot be fully appreciated without knowledge of its source (the title indicating that master text to be Murnau's film and not Stoker's book), allowing the movie-literate audience to re-experience many sequences by recalling nearly identical compositions and blocking. The total aesthetic effect goes far beyond the generic allusions to certain images (rats, cut fingers, ruined castles, abandoned ships) or dialogue ("I never drink . . . wine"); instead, Herzog has apparently conceived every moment with Murnau's original in mind, "bringing it to new life" as the "undead" inspiration—the phantom presence—behind his own creation. The parallel between his own art and his protagonist's vampirism could not have been far from his mind.

In contrast to Fisher's, Badham's, and Browning's adaptations, all three of which construct an animated, elegant, raven-haired, black-caped Count (the mass marketed image of Dracula so familiar in cartoons and Halloween masks) or Coppola's slightly stoned, long-haired, aging hippie lurking the London streets in blue-tinted spectacles and stovepipe hat (a cross between Charles Manson and John Lennon), Herzog's Nosferatu duplicates the somnambulistic, emaciated, bald-pated, and hollow-eyed figure first incarnated by Max Schreck. Kinski's performance thus brings to life a phantom of a phantom, a doubled double for the eternal isolation and ambiguity of human character that the cinema, with its particular mode of representing "lost objects," seems uniquely equipped to represent. Whereas Murnau's silent film projected the deceptive, disturbing, and evanescent aspect of character through such relatively new "tricks" as superimposition and negative shots, Herzog employs more subtle reflexive strategies to adumbrate the affinities between his central character and his medium. The result, as Lotte Eisner predicted after observing the shooting of *Nosferatu, the Vampyre*, extends the definition of a remake to something like Murnau's film "reborn" (Andrews 33).

MURNAU'S *NOSFERATU*

Through the vagaries of film history, *Nosferatu, a Symphony of Horror* had already been reborn—or at least restored—before Herzog undertook the project. According to John Barbow, the original negative of Murnau's classic has been lost; thus, the existing prints (now widely distributed in 16mm and video format) are *copies*, all of them incomplete, reproduced, from Murnau's shooting script and commentary (82). This circumstance compounds the usual ontological status of the film image as a "lost object" and a figure of the "undead." Even the literary characters have been displaced: Murnau's shooting script changes the names from Stoker's novel (for example, Dracula is called Count Orlock, Renfield is Knock), and different names are used in different prints of the film (for example, Jonathan's wife may be called Ellen or Nina).

In loosely adapting Stoker's novel to the screen,[20] Murnau simplified the social concerns while significantly expanding the role of the Count, making him the dominant character. "Stoker's novel tells of a serious struggle between human systems. The ending is a paean not only to the good and moral but also to the enlightened, social, domestic, and scientific culture of late nineteenth-century England" (Todd 200–01). Probably influenced by Freud (whose essay "The Uncanny" first appeared in 1919) and certainly by German Expressionism, Murnau's concerns are more psychological than social, as is evident in two ambiguous cuts between Nina and the far distant Count. In the first of these, while sleepwalking from her bedroom in Bremen, Nina calls out to Jonathan, who lies prostrate before the menacing shadow of the Count in his Carpathian castle. An intertitle says that Jonathan heard her warning cry, but the cross cut shows only Dracula retreating in apparent response. In a second sleepwalking sequence, Nina awakens to announce, "He is coming! I must go to him!" but her reference is ambiguous since it follows a shot, not of Jonathan returning by stagecoach, but of Dracula's ship at sea. Earlier, she had kept a vigil on the beach, supposedly for her husband (who had left Bremen by land), further suggesting that the film's truest marriage is between herself and the vampire. Indeed, Murnau's other principal transformation of the novel (aside from expanding the Count's role) involves making Nina, not Von Helsing, Nosferatu's primary antagonist. Whereas in the novel, the woman must be saved from the monster, in the film she willingly sacrifices herself to become his destroyer. Von Helsing, on the other hand, is reduced to offering ineffectual lectures on Venus's-flytraps. The many remaining minor characters in the book are similarly simplified or eliminated. In comparison to Stoker's extended social morality play, Murnau's *Nosferatu* becomes essentially a tragedy with three characters.

In another departure from the novel, Murnau's Count casts a menacing shadow as he stalks first Jonathan and later Nina. Stoker's Dracula, of course, casts no shadow or reflection. While striking in their abstraction of the vampire's horrific threat, these magnified shadows on blank walls also serve as reminders of the cinema's mode of representation. Sabine Hake has noted how early German film before Murnau was marked by "a kind of promotional self-referentiality that draws attention to the cinema and foregrounds its means" in order to "show audiences how to appreciate the cinema and its increasingly sophisticated products, how to deal with feelings of astonishment and disbelief, and how to gain satisfaction from the playful awareness of the apparatus and the simultaneous denial of its presence" (37–38). Writing in 1913 about the potential of these trick films to express precisely that uncanny aspect of human experience the cinema of realism had seemingly denied, Georg Lukacs eagerly anticipated "the great poet who . . . uses the fantastic quality which merely derives from adventitious technical factors for meaningful metaphysical and stylistic purposes" (cited in Prawer 115). Murnau continues this tradition of the "cinema of attractions" from the previous decade, although the reflexivity of *Nosferatu*, like that of the earlier films Hake describes, has little to do with a modernist questioning of the mode of representation. Instead, Murnau explores the technical means available for representing the phantom of character that, for him, lies at the center of the story. In his film, unlike Coppola's, the depths of Dracula's alienation and depravity remain unfathomed: nothing is to be learned of his ancestry, his philosophy, or his personal feelings. The mystery shrouding his character can only be approached indirectly, as in the grotesque shadows that signify his presence (fig. 14).

Murnau's use of other special effects—particularly the negative shot of the coach taking Harker through the forest to Dracula's castle and the superimpositions (double exposures) of the vampire's sudden spectral appearance—can be understood as similar demonstrations of the affinity between the cinema's method of signification involving the play of presence/absence and the ambiguous character of the film's protagonist. The negative image of the stagecoach, with its shrouded windows and horses, extends the haunting effect of Méliès's phantom hearse; the superimpositions seem to defy human corporeality and privilege the *unheimlich*. Even the vampire's ultimate extinction, his dematerialization as conveyed through stop action and a puff of smoke, suggests by metonymy the spontaneous combustion that threatens the film's own nitrate stock. Of course, such subtle implications may have been far from the director's conscious design, but it seems significant that Murnau employs a quite different repertoire of stylistic devices— notably camera movement and depth focus—when he comes to portray a more ordinary, "realistic," though equally fascinating, character in *The Last Laugh* (1924).

HERZOG'S *NOSFERATU*

In setting out to adapt Murnau's *Nosferatu*, Herzog has retained the basic plot and mise-en-scène while refining the reflexive and expressionistic elements. Despite one reviewer's description of *Nosferatu, the Vampyre* as "simply Murnau with colour and sound" (Strick 127), Bruce Kawin has more precisely noted how"no more than three shots are exactly the same in both films (allowing for the fact that Herzog's are in color)" (45). Paradoxically, this homage to the history of German cinema and to the director Herzog considers his country's greatest remains the most personal of all the Dracula films. While remaking Murnau's masterpiece, Herzog has also managed to remake Herzog, exploring the signature themes and stylistic elements that have established his place as one of the seminal artists of the New German Cinema.

Although it is difficult to conceive of a more "faithful" remake, *Nosferatu, the Vampyre* also alters and even subverts Murnau's original in some significant ways. The most prominent

FIGURE 14. *Nosferatu, a Symphony of Horror.* Courtesy Museum of Modern Art

changes involve both foregrounding the collapse of civilized society in the face of Nosferatu's invasion and elaborating the vampire's personal history and psychological motivation. The primary effect of these changes is to reverse the theme of Stoker's novel, the triumph of good over evil, and to undercut the sense of closure in Murnau's film. In Herzog's romantic, subversive ending, Nosferatu lives on in the vampirized character of Jonathan Harker, who flees from the bourgeois town of Wismar (actually Delft) into what Metz might call a "primordial *elsewhere*," announcing that "I have much to do." Like the epilogue Polanski attaches to his adaptation of *Macbeth* (1971), this added scene expresses the director's personal reconception of the thematic implications of the original, an updating of the classic text in response to the exigencies of modern culture. The restoration of order in Shakespeare's and Murnau's work has been superseded by Polanski's and Herzog's vision of chronic malignancy.

Herzog's specific transformations of Murnau's *Nosferatu* may be organized according to a tripartite taxonomy of adaptation strategies broadly derived from Vladimir Propp: simplification, expansion, substitution (Crabbe 47). By eliminating the diary frame (the account of the plague in Wismar by one John Cavillus), Herzog excises the voice of rational authority over the progress of the story and replaces it with the mysterious choral accompaniment of Popul Vuh on the sound track. This simplification has the same effect as would cutting the frame story from *The Cabinet of Dr. Caligari*, thereby restoring the screenwriters' original subversive intent. Similarly, Dr. Von Helsing's scientific lectures have been eliminated, further undercutting any "objective" explanation for the film's irrational events. Herzog's expansions involve the development both of Dracula's more sympathetic character and of Wismar's more stifling, ineffectual society. In his silent film, Murnau could only suggest the Count's enervated, alienated existence through Schreck's performance and occasional cross cutting; Herzog adds dialogue expressing the vampire's world-weariness after witnessing centuries of sorrow,[21] and Kinski speaks in a labored whisper, as if he were breathing through a respirator. Most notoriously, Herzog expands the representation of pestilence by importing thousands of laboratory rats and turning them loose in the town square (antithetical to Stoker's reaffirmation of Victorian society and quite different from Murnau's orderly scenes showing crosses being painted on quarantined houses and coffins being carried through the streets). In preparation for his pessimistic ending, Herzog substitutes an ominous prelude for Murnau's initial images of domestic bliss (Jonathan picking flowers, Nina playing with her kitten). Thus, the credit sequence of *Nosferatu, the Vampyre* begins with a sustained tracking shot in a cave of contorted mummies, accompanied by a medieval dirge sung by Popul Vuh and followed by slow motion footage of a bat in flight. In the film's first diegetic scene, instead of tenderly receiving a bouquet from her husband, Lucy Harker awakens from a nightmare.

These transformations confirm Herzog's assertion that he is not simply remaking *Nosferatu* but revivifying it. As in all previous versions, however, there remains at the very center of his film the haunting figure of Dracula himself, constructed here as the mysterious object of both fear and desire. Reflecting another crucial change from its predecessors, the climax of *Nosferatu, the Vampyre* depicts Lucy drawing the vampire back to her neck as he begins to withdraw with the arrival of dawn. The bedside tableau clearly portrays the erotic subtext left imperfectly concealed in earlier versions of the story—and rampant in Coppola's adaptation. In this moment, Dracula transcends his previous incarnations as moral monster to become the double of Harker (who first appears whispering words of comfort into his frightened wife's neck as she awakens from her nightmare), the alter ego of Herzog (who identifies with the vampire's romantic restlessness), and the phantom of the cinema.

There are phantoms everywhere in Herzog's text. In addition to the presiding spirit of Murnau and Kinski's reincarnation of Schreck, *Nosferatu, the Vampyre* conjures up the ghost of Stoker by restoring his original characters' names and echoes Bela Lugosi's famous line from Browning's *Dracula* (also found in the novel) when the Count responds to the cry of wolves: "Listen! The children of the night make their music." Roland Topor's performance as Renfield, which drew mixed responses from reviewers, seems more comprehensible when understood as an allusion to the stylized appearances of Peter Lorre in dozens of horror films. Herzog thus evokes the history of what Eisner called Germany's "haunted screen," in addition to referring to German painting (Caspar David Friedrich's mountain landscapes and ruined castles) and music (the Wagnerian soundtrack). Finally, Herzog resurrects the ghost of Herzog in a number of ways that recall his own earlier films: the repertory company of collaborators, including Kinski, Popul Vuh, and cinematographer Jorg Schmidt-Reitwein; the time-lapse landscape shots as the clouds move over the mountains from *Heart of Glass*

(1976); the panning shots of Nosferatu's raft on the river from *Aguirre, Wrath of God* (1972); the slow motion depiction of the bat's flight from *The Great Ecstasy of the Woodsculptor Steiner* (1974); the alienated protagonist and impotent bureaucrats from *The Mystery of Kaspar Hauser* (1974). By such varied means does the film continually inscribe presence/absence as a way of representing the aura of the vampire as well as the undying appeal of the remake, which leaves the spectator continuously aware of the existence of an earlier model that is both different and (with the exception of inserted footage, as in *The Spirit of the Beehive* [1973]) absent from the present text.

In *Nosferatu, the Vampyre,* Herzog provides several occasions of presence/absence within the diegesis, discovering more subtle means for depicting a world of "lost objects" and the "undead" than Murnau's exploitation of stock effects such as negative shots and stop action. The film's arresting pre-credit sequence, with its slow tracking across the stricken faces of the mummified dead, begins to evoke the phantom netherworld that every film—but especially this film—brings to life. In addition to his relentlessly moving camera, Herzog employs an expressionist sound track—a mournful two-note requiem combined with the amplified sound of a heartbeat creating an aural figure of absence/presence—to animate the still images, rendering them as "undead" through the particular signifying elements of the cinema. Similarly, the closing time-lapse shot of Harker riding off into the distance across a desert landscape accompanied by the choral strains of Gounod's *Sanctus* confirms his new identity as a lost soul destined to wander eternally in a virtual elsewhere and elsewhen. But the question of character remains: Has Harker's identity been permanently *transformed* by the vampire's bite, or simply *revealed*?

Another privileged moment that suggests the cinema's potential to represent the uncanny occurs when Harker seeks transport across the Borgo Pass to Dracula's castle. Herzog invents a dialogue scene missing from Murnau's silent film. While attending his four horses hitched to the stagecoach, the coachman replies to Jonathan's request for passage, "I haven't any coach." Asked if he will sell one of the horses in plain view for double the price, he answers, "Can you not see? I haven't any horses."[22] After walking alone for days across the mountains, Harker is finally rescued by the mysterious appearance of another coach, whose driver (as in both Murnau and Browning) disappears before they reach the castle. In a third permutation of what might be understood as a kind of reincarnation of Méliès's phantom hearse, the stricken Harker is driven back to Wismar in a single horse rig whose perfectly balanced reflection Herzog mirrors in the adjacent canal. In each case the imaginary calls into question, in effect remakes, the real.

In addition to such conventional devices as mirror shots and dramatic shadows, Herzog often employs formal composition within the frame to create negative space, most prominently in the domestic scenes in Wismar after Harker's return. In one shot-in-depth, for example, Lucy reads a book about Dracula in close-up while her debilitated husband can be glimpsed in the background slumped in a chair, now truly a lost soul barely distinguishable from the furniture. A more subtle use of mise-en-scène occurs earlier at the mountain inn. Harker impatiently demands his dinner so that he can be on his way to the Count's castle. At the mention of Dracula's name, the gypsies all suddenly stop eating, and the composition becomes a virtual freeze frame. In the foreground with his back to the camera, Jonathan confronts the silent, crowded room, with diners on either side of the frame and a triangular shadow in the middle ground pointing towards an empty window at the vanishing point. In this possible allusion to Renaissance paintings of the Last Supper, Herzog emphasizes not the presence of the Savior, but the absence of communion: Jonathan remains estranged from both the innkeeper behind him (and the camera) and the guests before him; there is no chalice, no food, nothing in the window but a foreboding vacancy. Herzog follows this sequence with more obvious parodies of the Last Supper: first, when Jonathan dines with Dracula at the castle and later when the rats replace the bourgeois party consuming their "last supper" in the ruined town square.

These various phantom figures—the transmogrified mummies, the uncertain coaches, the debilitated husband, the empty window—all suggest a connection between the vampire's elusive, nocturnal existence and the cinema's representation of character. As Nosferatu drains his victims of blood, the film image deprives its referent of the materiality it once possessed when it appeared before the camera. Every object, every actor becomes a ghost in the moment of projection, but, as I have argued earlier, no object seems as slippery, duplicitous, and evanescent as human character, that subjectivity which must remain both partially hidden (character as a signified, a combination of emotional, moral, and cognitive traits) and vulnerable to change. Herzog, a filmmaker conversant with contemporary critical theory, intensifies the spectator's awareness of this "lost object" status of his medium through a number of reflexive moments, some of which have already been described. The prominent mirror images, for example—Lucy's reflection in the water during her sleepwalking, the horizontal tracking shot of the coach returning Jonathan to Wismar, and the powerful scene when Dracula first visits Lucy as she sits before her dressing mirror—serve as reminders of the camera's mimetic function as well as the Lacanian basis ("the mirror stage") for Metz's theory of cinema's imaginary signifier. Following Murnau's example in defying Stoker's conception of Dracula as casting no shadow, Herzog's Nosferatu is virtually defined by the darkness in which he lives and which he casts over others. In a brilliant stroke, Herzog displays only the Count's shadow entering Lucy's bedroom and reflecting in her mirror, the door opening as if by itself; as he advances on her frightened form doubled in the glass, he casts no reflection of his own. Like Lucy, then, the terrified spectator contemplates the *framed reflection of a shadow*. What has been signified in this tableau, the irreconcilable aspects of power and vulnerability inherent in Dracula's character (here he begs only to share Lucy's love), has been perfectly matched by the cinematic representation.

At times, in fact, Herzog's Nosferatu almost stands in for the cinema itself. In the memorable long shot of his phosphorescent skull glimmering in the darkened upper window of his Wismar mansion—a shot borrowed directly from Murnau—he resembles the light from the projection booth, casting his gaze on the community (in Wismar, in the theater) he holds in thrall (fig. 15). This association also occurs earlier at the castle when the Count serves Harker a midnight supper. Dracula sits above and behind his visitor, his white bulb of a head surrounded by darkness and framed by a window, his menacing shadow cast on the wall, his labored breath like the sound of the projector mechanism, his attentive guest increasingly menaced by his mesmerizing presence (fig. 16). Judith Mayne has aptly described how Nosferatu here occupies "a literal 'no man's land'" (126) in the black background of the composition, the same uncharted region Harker himself will traverse in the film's concluding vision when he becomes, in effect, the remake of his master.

Perhaps the sanctification of the vampire's continuing mission as enunciated in the finale by Gounod's chorus should not be regarded as simply ironic. Like Herzog remaking Murnau, Harker as the new Nosferatu has not only escaped the quotidian realm that

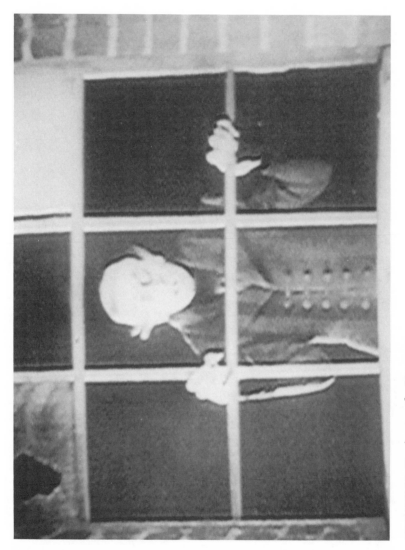

FIGURE 15. *Nosferatu, the Vampyre*

FIGURE 16. *Nosferatu, the Vampyre.* Courtesy Museum of Modern Art

FIGURE 17. *Nosferatu, the Vampyre*

first oppressed him ("These canals that go nowhere but back on themselves," as Jonathan had described Wismar) but also transcended his mentor's fate (fig. 17). No wonder, then, that Herzog seems to celebrate his disappearance into myth, to be reborn again in each new screening as the phantom of the cinema.

CHAPTER FIVE

◈

The Spy and the Cipher

If the movie monster may fairly be described as a figure of excess—physical excess in most cases, such as Frankenstein's creature, the Wolf Man, King Kong, and Godzilla, but also excessive desire in the generic versions of the vampire—these frightening representations of character run amuck may also be considered doubles for the "cinema of attractions," sites of a spectacle readily comprehensible as imposing, material, and evil. Lurking in the shadows of this spectacle, burdened by the light, are the indeterminate and therefore more haunting figures of Murnau's and Herzog's Nosferatus. The character types I consider next, the spy and the cipher, become interesting as representative human beings and not literally "agents" of ideology (Western democracy as protected by James Bond or innocent pastoralism as expressed by Chance in *Being There*) when they are constructed to reflect the furtiveness and insubstantiality of the film image that the commercial industry ("the apparatus," as Baudry broadly conceives it) typically seeks to overcome through spectacle. In these less common texts, they become doubles of the cinematic "lack," representatives of a kind of un-being.

By now the outlines of my argument for the significance of the protagonists of these films should be clear: as elusive representatives of both the cinema's signifying system and of the idea of enigmatic personhood attached to certain people encountered in real life, they embody both the modernist conception of fractured, irrecoverable identity and the postmodernist vision of a constantly mediated, illusory existence. As with the horror genre, very few spy films have concentrated on the complex motives and ambiguous moral concerns that comprise the spy's personal character; instead, as illustrated by the James Bond series that has become almost a genre unto itself, the conflict centers on the clearly defined forces of good and evil, while the cartoonish protagonist is known almost exclusively by his acts of derring-do. In short, this kind of spy film has become a subcategory of the action/adventure movie.

John le Carré's novels, beginning with *Call for the Dead* (1961), have served to revive the tradition of serious espionage fiction begun by Joseph Conrad and extending through Graham Greene[23] and to inspire a number of successful film adaptations for both theatrical (*The Spy Who Came in from the Cold* [1965], *The Little Drummer Girl* [1984], *The Russia House* [1990]) and televised (*Tinker, Tailor, Soldier, Spy* [1980], *Smiley's People* [1982], *A Perfect Spy* [1987]) distribution. Because le Carré's books explore the grimy deceptions, petty betrayals, and pervasive disillusionment of Cold War espionage while portraying the spy as an ordinary, compulsive, and confused "technician," as Leamus describes himself in *The Spy Who Came in from the Cold*, they have been praised for lifting the genre to new levels of realism (le Carré was himself employed for many years by British intelligence) and for restoring "the novel of action into a novel of character and motivation" (Monaghan xi). Leamus's monologue near the end of Martin Ritt's film adaptation succinctly defines le Carré's spy as a modern anti-hero:

> What the hell do you think spies are? Moral philosophers measuring everything they do against the word of God or Karl Marx? They're not. They're just a bunch of seedy, squalid bastards like me. Little men, drunkards, queers, henpecked husbands. Civil servants playing cowboys-and-Indians to brighten their rotten little lives. Do you think they sit like monks in a cell balancing right against wrong?

Enunciated by Richard Burton, these lines taken directly from the novel[24] ring with an almost Shakespearean profundity.

In le Carré's fiction, the spy's character is measured against not only his Cold War adversaries beyond the iron curtain (Fiedler in *The Spy Who Came in from the Cold*, Karla in *Smiley's People*, to choose perhaps the most vivid examples) but also the British intelligence bureaucracy known collectively as "The Circus" and individually through "moles" like Bill Hayden (*Tinker, Tailor, Soldier, Spy*), factotums like Peter Guillam (*The Honourable Schoolboy*), burnt-out cases like Magnus Pym (*A Perfect Spy*), and the nameless chief of London operations known as Control. His novels deliberately obscure the issue of which side holds the greater threat to the protagonist. The spy's triumphs are often hollow, his ultimate defeat—by the forces of foreign intrigue or domestic betrayal (personal and professional)—inevitable. At bottom, he is a counterfeit. "Even when you are telling the truth, you lie," his dear comrade says to Magnus Pym, the title character of *A Perfect Spy*. "You have loyalty and affection. But to what? To whom?" (432). The same questions lie at the heart of the twelve-part, thirteen-hour made-for-television film *Reilly: Ace of Spies* (1984).

In addition to the element of mystery shrouding its protagonist, *Reilly*'s detailed evocation of a relatively distant, misunderstood historical period (before and after the Russian Revolution), its large cast of generally unfamiliar actors in complex roles, its unusually dense visual field (in contrast to the "talking heads" design favored by television), and its literate script seem influenced more by the European art cinema than by commercial television practice, although it remains a rather unique hybrid of the two forms. More than any feature film produced for theatrical distribution, *Reilly* focusses on the unknowable identity of the spy, preserving the integrity of his character, like that of Zinnemann's Jackal, despite the moral repugnance of his behavior. And more than any televised representation of the spy, excepting the three BBC adaptations of le Carré's novels, it maintains the dense mise-en-scène, complicated plot, and subtle secondary roles associated with serious cinematic texts.

REILLY: ACE OF SPIES

The sheer length of a mini-series like *Reilly: Ace of Spies* or the numerous adaptations of classic novels aired on *Masterpiece Theatre* and its imitators would seem to assure the full presentation of character associated with the great works of nineteenth-century fiction, many of which were themselves serialized for their original audiences. Certainly *Reilly* shares with the majority of artistically conceived narratives shown on public television stations or produced for cable outlets an historical scope and richness along with attentiveness to period details, a theatrically trained cast featuring a dozen or more distinguished supporting roles, a fluid cinematic style, picturesque and often exotic settings, and a lush yet unobtrusive musical score. What sets this particular film apart, however, remains its sustained focus on a protagonist who, like a true master spy, persistently frustrates the efforts of both his associates and audiences to fix his identity. In this respect, Reilly embodies the play of presence/absence installed by the text's status as a film but complicated by its transmission on television, whose predominant myth is that of immediacy (Ellis 77). When we further consider the voyeuristic element of the spy's activity, which often involves taking pictures or conveying microfilm, the connection between the ontology of the medium and the elusiveness of the character becomes clearer still.

In contrast to the obfuscating rhetoric of *Reilly*'s construction of character, Neil Postman has pointed out how television's usual practice of presentation has evolved toward condensation and simplification: "Every television program must be a complete package in itself. No previous knowledge is required" (147). While this formula has recently changed with the introduction of continuous narratives on a few programs such as *Murder One*, it remains generally valid for commercial mini-series and prestigious adaptations alike. Characters remain essentially flat and static in order to be readily recalled from week to week. Thus, in a contemporary production like *The Jewel in the Crown* (1984), which seems otherwise comparable to *Reilly: Ace of Spies*, the audience's interest is maintained from week to week by the immediately recognizable main characters such as the maimed, villainous Merrick and the compassionate, intelligent Sarah.

Reilly's character, however, appears evanescent and in flux. Perhaps to compensate for the opacity of his central figure, writer Troy Kennedy Martin has created a tripartite structure that encourages a subtle but discernible shift in the general perception of the protagonist. Drawing on the audience's familiarity with James Bond in particular, Martin begins with a man who seems at first a conventional romantic figure. In the early episodes, he has said, "I posit the idea that Reilly believes he can right the world by being an agent" (Billington 27), and so his character accomplishes a succession of political and amorous conquests while the text also suggests certain cynical and mercenary motives meant to be anomalous with the popular film image of the spy as embodied by James Bond. In part three ("The Visiting Fireman"), these unheroic elements assume greater prominence, as Reilly confounds his superiors and willfully betrays a youthful fellow agent in order to manipulate a brilliant but cold-hearted coup. Subsequent episodes reveal him to be a compulsive womanizer and fanatical opportunist, partially redeemed only by the audience's growing awareness of the corruption that marks the worlds—Whitehall, Berlin, Moscow—he inhabits. The moral ambivalence aroused by his isolation, ruthlessness, and apparent solipsism is similar to the effect created by le Carré's portrait of the modern spy or Shakespeare's deliberate withdrawal of sympathy for the tragic hero in the fourth acts of *Macbeth* and *Hamlet*. In the end, though, Reilly emerges as a man spurred on by a counter-revolutionary political mission (like Hamlet) and extraordinary personal courage (like Macbeth) who is defeated in his ultimate aims both by his own overreaching and by times distinctly out of joint.

In a further effort to unravel the mystery of the real-life character, the original American telecast of *Reilly: Ace of Spies* offered introductory commentary by Vincent Price from *Gorey Mansion*, the set for the PBS series *Mystery*. These remarks serve to frame each episode by providing pertinent if simplified historical and political information, much in line with both public broadcasting's "educational" origins and the function of voiceover narration in traditional documentary films. Thus, Price introduces the first program by telling us that "the nineteenth century seemed to spawn men who were larger than life." He then recalls how Ian Fleming dismissed his own fictional creation, James Bond, when compared to Sidney Reilly. At the beginning of episode two, Price describes Reilly as "a man who thrived on danger, a man who had knowledge of many countries and languages." Such fervid language and repeated references to James Bond construct the protagonist as a swashbuckling romantic hero who also happened to be, in Price's words, "the greatest espionage agent who ever lived."

In sharp contrast to Price's typically histrionic, clichéd presentations for the American audience, the film itself provides an unseen narrator (Michael Bryant) who supplies limited expositional details (usually at the beginning and sometimes at the conclusion of each segment) concerning the political climate or the outcome of historical events Reilly has set in motion, but who never explicates the protagonist's psychological makeup. Bryant's tone is always literate, subdued, and morally neutral. While Price describes how the older Reilly "blindly believed' the social revolutionaries in his "persistent obsession" to overthrow the Bolsheviks at the beginning of part nine ("After Moscow"), the narrator remarks at the end of the same episode: "Despite the personal ties which Reilly still retained with the [British] Service, his future now lay with Boris Savinkoff and the Russian émigré movement." The dialectical tension between these two commentaries rather clearly demonstrates the discrepancy between classical Hollywood's typical construction of character as a spectacle of traits (exemplified perfectly by Vincent Price's own lengthy screen career) and the phantom figure that calls into question such over-determined representations.

The first episode of *Reilly: Ace of Spies* ("An Affair with a Married Woman") draws most heavily on the movies' James Bond by presenting a handsome international adventurer both irresistible to women and beyond the traditions of the British Secret Service. Set in Baku, Russia, in 1901, the story concerns Reilly's smuggling Russian surveys of the Persian oil basin and his seduction of a young English woman married to an aged, sickly clergyman. As played by the then unknown Australian actor Sam Neill (who subsequently became a finalist in the search to replace Roger Moore as James Bond), Reilly cunningly manipulates four separate parties: Margaret Thomas (Jeananne Crowley), the vulnerable lady who will become his first wife, soon his albatross; the Russian captain who guards him under house arrest and likens him to Prometheus, "thief of secrets"; Basil Zaharov (Leo McKern), the international arms dealer who will be Reilly's antagonist throughout the first six episodes; and perhaps most tellingly, Chief Cummings (Norman Addway), head of British Intelligence, who describes Reilly as "a pimp and a murderer . . . probably a socialist and certainly a Jew." Cummings's regard for his most successful agent will gradually change during the thirteen-hour film; indeed, his judgment of Reilly—along with that of his subordinate, Major Fothergill (Peter Egan)—generally functions as a barometer of the audience's own shifting comprehension.

Reilly's ingenious triumphs over all four potential adversaries, combined with his suave grace under pressure (dressed in evening clothes, he dines and gambles with his guard at a table set in the street), initially suggest a conventional television hero as well as James Bond, but this first episode also provides certain anomalous details. For one, Reilly abandons Margaret in Baku, exposing her to the deprivations of nineteen weeks in a Russian prison, the recriminations of her perverse husband, and the merciless scrutiny of the British press. When she finally confronts her lover back in London, he replies with what Cummings rightly characterizes as scandalously unheroic indifference:

M: You manipulated me in the most cynical manner.
R: I had to use whatever method I could to get out.

Reilly's sole allegiance at this stage appears to be to a whore, Rose McConnell, who also serves as his messenger to Whitehall (thus, presumably, Cummings's "pimp" remark). When Rose is accidentally killed by one of Zaharov's clumsy henchmen, Reilly swears vengeance and is deeply moved. That night, alone in his room—for the only time in the series—Reilly weeps.

Episode two ("Prelude to War") continues to undermine the idea of an invulnerable romantic hero in its portrayal of Reilly conspiring on Whitehall's orders with the Japanese navy as it prepares to attack Port Arthur, thereby beginning the Russo-Japanese War. First (according to Price's introduction), Reilly deliberately works against his homeland, Russia, apparently because he can reap huge profits by speculating in coal and other war material. "It's a bad situation," he drily remarks, "but I don't see why we shouldn't make any money out of it." Second, he seems totally indifferent to Margaret's unhappiness, her affair with a young shipping clerk, her incipient alcoholism, or her pleas for his attention. Finally, after making plans with the Japanese invaders to abandon the port, he is spurned by his friend Captain Macdougal, whom he has entrusted with evacuating Margaret before the attack begins. In a chilling farewell whose impact directly contradicts the customary sympathy for the hero, the old sailor tells Reilly, "I doubt that we shall meet again, but if we do, it will no longer be as friends." While this episode begins with a low angle shot of Reilly astride a white horse in majestic silhouette and ends with his complete political success, his character no longer conforms to any preconceived notion of the romantic adventurer. He has become, for the time being, a mercenary.

In the crucial third installment, and throughout the middle episodes, the amalgam of ruthlessness, isolation, and unprincipled genius in Reilly's character remains foregrounded. Price's introduction, playing off his own malevolent persona, proclaims the protagonist "menacing, audacious, an egomaniac and sinister." Although he never quite descends to pure villainy—he is, after all, working for the British, here against Germany—Reilly never appears less sympathetic than in "The Visiting Fireman."

The scene is Hamburg, 1905, the Blohm and Voss shipyards; Reilly's mission is to relieve a beleaguered young agent, Goshen (Bill Nighy), and to steal the plans for the latest German battleship.

Significantly, in light of his increasingly ambiguous characterization, Reilly appears—for the first time—*disguised* as a rough, unshaven worker named "Fricker." Thus, his "true" nature further retreats behind the persona he had adopted in changing his name from "Rosenberg" to "Reilly" upon marrying Margaret and apparently joining the Establishment into a theatrically conceived new identity, an outsider's role he plays with relish as well as great skill. In swift succession, Fricker manages to secure a rented room with the unsuspecting Goshen, seduce the landlord's daughter, ingratiate himself with the German agent, von Jaeger, who is charged with apprehending the suspected British spy, and most important, intercept Cummings's letters alerting Goshen that help is on the way, fearing that the unhinged agent will give them both away. Reilly's equivocal position is dramatized when Fothergill arrives to bring him in line:

F: Our tradition demands that we do not let our men down in the field.
R: But you do it all the time, old boy.

In the very next scene, Fricker destroys another letter to Goshen.

While Reilly's betrayal of his fellow agent is certainly disturbing, the film also acknowledges (later on) the truth of his accusation against the Service, a strong theme throughout le Carré's espionage fiction. In the previous episode, for example, Whitehall has betrayed its ally, Russia, by ordering Reilly to meet with the Japanese navy. And it will be Britain's refusal to supply sufficient troops for a landing at Archangel in 1918 that will sabotage Reilly's own plans to overthrow the Bolsheviks in the most critical action of his entire career. When Goshen, at the end of his tether, is trapped by von Jaeger atop a shipyard tower, his confession indicts both his superiors in London and, without his ever knowing it, Reilly as well: "I've been most unfairly treated, and my trust has been abused, and I've been misled." With a mob of workers, Fricker among them, chanting "Spy! Spy!" on the docks below, Goshen plunges to his death, victim of the fallen world that Reilly so skillfully navigates. After killing the landlord and abandoning his daughter in making his escape, Reilly next appears clean-shaven, immaculately dressed, smoking a cigar with Basil Zaharov on the train back to England.

The contrasting commentaries of the two narrators at the conclusion of "The Visiting Fireman" provide alternative characterizations. The film's voiceover takes the long view, defining as always the protagonist's historical role: "With the return of Goshen's body, a new realism entered the British intelligence service, not only because of their growing rivalry with Germany but because they now began to learn from Reilly's ruthless approach." Price's closing remarks for television rather cloyingly seek to re-establish Reilly's heroic stature, which the preceding fifty minutes have relentlessly deconstructed. He describes how the film's climactic close-up of von Jaeger staring at the transformed "Fricker," now at Fothergill's side officially receiving Goshen's coffin, conveys "unspoken admiration for the man who had so completely outwitted him." While such a look of silent recognition may be subject to varied interpretation, von Jaeger's expression seems to reveal less admiration than contempt.

Parts four through six, which take place largely inside Russia, encompass Reilly's final abandonment of Margaret and subsequent bigamous marriage to a Russian countess, his incestuous relationship with his long-lost sister Anna (whom he had also abandoned years before), his ambiguous career representing German shipping interests, and his ultimate triumph over Zaharov at the 1910 St. Petersburg "Arms Sale of the Century," thereby restoring the Russian fleet he had helped the Japanese to destroy at Port Arthur. A kind of Wandering Jew (born Sigmund Rosenberg in Odessa, an illegitimate offspring of his mother's affair with her Jewish doctor) motivated by a "cockeyed morality" according to Cummings and a "cold hearted bastard" in the words of his fun-loving Russian companion Sasha Grammatikoff (Brian Protheride), he evolves into an amalgam of Ian Fleming's sophisticated womanizer, James Bond, and John le Carré's brilliant survivor, George Smiley, but more ruthless than the former and less phlegmatic than the latter. The essential indeterminacy of his character is perhaps best conveyed in a brief sequence from part five that cuts from a three-shot of Sasha and two lively women in the back seat of a carriage to their companion for the evening's party, Reilly, surrounded by darkness and probing for more information to further his latest scheme. Now the hit of St. Petersburg society, dressed in beautiful suits and winning at cards against royalty, he has nevertheless merely exchanged his disguise as Fricker for one more respectable.

The rehabilitation of Reilly's character begins with the immediate aftermath of the Russian Revolution. "Motivated by personal conviction," as Price explains, and with the financial backing of the British government, he plots the overthrow of Lenin. "Reilly was one of a dozen like-minded Allied officers who were determined to remove the Bolshevik leader," the film's voiceover narration explains, "but he was the only one to consider placing himself at the head of a new government." Throughout this period, "Captain" Reilly wears the cap and leather jacket of the Flying Corps, a uniform that subtly associates him with the heroic "flying leather-necks" of numerous Hollywood war movies (fig. 18). At this point, the audience's regard for the protagonist is further influenced by its understanding of two historical facts: the failure of the counter-revolution and the tyranny and deepening antagonism toward the West of Soviet Communism. Thus, Reilly's efforts are simultaneously perceived as undertaken on behalf of a loftier political ideal and ultimately doomed. Like the tragic hero, in other words, he has been born to set things right and to suffer the slings and arrows of outrageous fortune. The film dramatizes this poignant fate at the conclusion of part eight ("Endgame") when, following the collapse of his elaborate conspiracy and the execution of political friends, Reilly quietly acknowledges his defeat to George Hill, Cummings's agent in Moscow:

R: I thought I'd done it. I really thought I had it in my hand.
H: You did, old boy.

The remaining four episodes of *Reilly: Ace of Spies* seem marked by entropy, the protagonist's vulnerability and anti-Bolshevism (understood, of course, as anticommunism) eliciting the requisite pity and fear at his impending fate.

Part nine ("After Moscow") begins this long denouement. While it depicts the protagonist in yet another amorous relationship and culminates in his exciting escape from an assassination attempt, the episode remains doubly burdened by memory of Reilly's failed coup and anticipation of his inevitable end. Even his old nemesis, Chief Cummings, has mellowed toward him. In this segment, Reilly seems adrift and vulnerable on several scores:

1. he has been sentenced in absentia for his role in the plot to overthrow Lenin;
2. he has been borrowing money throughout Europe to support the morphine addict Savinkoff;
3. he is attacked by the British Foreign Office for abandoning the embassy in Moscow and taking off with the navy's money loaned to the anti-Bolshevik cause;

FIGURE 18. *Reilly: Ace of Spies*. Courtesy Thames Television

4. he is driven to seek the help of a seer, Caryll Houselander (Joanne Pearce), to divine some vision of his friend Mary Freed's last hours in Moscow's Lubianka prison;
5. he is pursued by a hired assassin.

Yet Reilly will not yield. Confronted with Caryll Houselander's sketches prophesying his own lonely death in the snowy fields outside Moscow, he suffers, unlike Macbeth, no momentary loss of nerve. He invites the assassin, Adamson, in for a drink. "There is a weakness in you," Adamson tells him. "It surprises me, but it's there." Reilly coldly replies, "Don't count on it, my friend." Even his lovely new mistress, Alexandra (called "the Plugger")—a charming, self-proclaimed whore, at least so long as the war is still on—serves finally to underscore her lover's profound isolation. True to her word, she becomes the first woman willingly to leave him, prompting this haunting farewell:

R: I can't persuade you to stay?
A: I said that when the war is over I'd go back to mother . . . Good luck, though I can't help feeling you're living on borrowed time.

As Reilly begins to recede into myth, the film adopts a distinctly elegiac tone, all the more poignant for the similarities between the unpretentious, witty Alexandra and his first love, Rose McConnell.

The narrative ends on what seems a fitting note of indeterminacy. As with Reilly's early years, including a stint in South America, historians remain uncertain about the circumstances surrounding his death. Troy Kennedy Martin's script follows closely the careful documentation of Robin Bruce Lockhart's biography, but where the book ends with various conflicting accounts of the spy's capture and execution inside Russia, the film opts for the conventional narrative continuity of television drama by offering only one version, entirely Martin's invention: Reilly deliberately leaves himself open to arrest in order to discredit the supposedly anti-Bolshevik organization called "The Trust," actually a shadow group invented by Reilly's antagonist throughout the second half of the series, Felix Dzerjinsky (Tom Bell), head of the Soviet Cheka. While Reilly's motives in undertaking this fatal journey back to his homeland remain mysterious (with some historians asserting that he was probably a Soviet double agent all along), the film ascribes Shakespearean dimensions to his conduct: like Hamlet, he seeks revenge for the deaths of Mary Freed and Boris Savinkoff; like Macbeth, he fights on despite advance knowledge of his fate; like Othello, in the borrowed words Cummings employs when defending his agent before the prime minister, "he has done the state some service."

The scene depicting his execution visually expresses the motif of presence/absence that is the spy's *métier*. Dzerjinsky accompanies Reilly into an open field surrounded by woods. They reminisce about "the old days" before the Revolution until Felix stops midway in their walk and tells his prisoner, "I leave you now." These, the last words Reilly hears on earth, echo the film's theme of abandonment, but they also reaffirm the infinite elusiveness of the protagonist, who leaves *us* now without having revealed the secrets of his character. From an unseen, distant position a rifle shot rings out, and a high-angle long shot leaves us to contemplate Reilly's body in the snow, positioned exactly as Caryll Houselander had sketched him. After a brief epilogue scene, the film dissolves to this final image, the corpse now partially covered with snow.

NOTES ON THE CIPHER:
ZELIG AND *THE MYSTERY OF KASPAR HAUSER*

With the exception of this closing shot, which slowly conceals the figure of Reilly without removing all trace, *Reilly: Ace of Spies* does not reflexively display the film image's play of presence/absence in order to reinforce the fugitive character of the spy. *Reilly* is unusual, however, in its constantly shifting perspective on the ostensible hero's moral and ideological position.[25] Like all successful spies, Reilly is a chameleon, ever changing his social roles and political allegiances but, like the deceptive scorpion of the fable that frames the narrative of another changeable character in Neil Jordan's *The Crying Game* (1992), always true to his own hidden nature.

Woody Allen's *Zelig* (1983) portrays a "chameleon man" of a different sort, a cipher in search of an essence to which to be true, more in line with le Carré's portraits of the modern spy. Zelig's pathology, manifested in his uncanny transformations in order to blend in with the people around him, reflects not the spy's habitual distrust of others, however, but an ontological insecurity, a mistrust of *self*. In his marvelous manipulations of documentary footage, Allen and his collaborators re-invent the cinema of attractions and literally inscribe the character—Leonard Zelig, cultural icon of the 1920s, but also Woody Allen, the actor who impersonates this pseudo-historical figure—onto the surface of the film. While contemporary intellectuals including Susan Sontag, Saul Bellow, Irving Howe, and Bruno Bettelheim pose alternative responses to the voiceover narrator's central question, "Who *was* this Leonard Zelig?" the protagonist himself appears only as a black-and-white image captured in still photographs, newsreels, and home movies.[26] In the therapeutic "White Room Sessions" recorded by the hidden cameraman, Paul Deghuee, Zelig is induced by his psychiatrist, Dr. Eudora Fletcher (Mia Farrow), to resist his conformist compulsion only to be revealed as a man "devoid of personality," made small and vulnerable by the detached, distant, and fixed lens. In a clever development of this reflexive sequence, Allen presents scenes from a fictitious 1935 Warner Bros. biopic, *The Changing Man*, that parody Hollywood's facile efforts at reconstructing and comprehending historical characters. Because the actors who impersonate Zelig and Dr. Fletcher are such idealized representatives of the "real" persons recorded in the newsreels, the movie merely obfuscates the mystery of the cipher's "unstable makeup" while presuming to resolve it. *Zelig* thus becomes a kind of comic inversion of *Citizen Kane*. Written and directed by its immediately recognizable star performer, concerned with issues of celebrity, mass behavior, and media power, *Zelig*'s central theme is again the enigma posed by a man's life, in this case the life of a nonentity rather than a giant; its narrative structure again involves the accumulation of different perspectives, in this case primarily from non-diegetic, real life witnesses rather than diegetic, fictional characters; its formal inventiveness again involves the editing of historical images, in this case with implications that are ludicrous rather than portentous.

Werner Herzog's *The Mystery of Kaspar Hauser* (*Every Man for Himself and God Against All* [1975]) presents an interesting contrast to *Zelig* by centering on an actual historical character, an apparently dim-witted foundling of indeterminate age who suddenly appeared in Nuremberg in 1828 after having spent his life in a dark cellar and who became a celebrity after publishing his autobiography. Like the eccentric Zelig, Kaspar Hauser comes to represent the spirit of his age through his metamorphosis from wild child to socialized man (Peucker 181). But Herzog chooses to present his narrative in a visionary rather than documentary style that aligns the spectator with the protagonist's unique view of nature rather than educated society's view of him. Zelig's transformations and unexpected appearances, while mildly satiric, serve mainly to underscore the movie's technical virtuosity. Herzog's film seems more ambitious. Beyond his status as an object for Romantic theories and aristocratic entertainment ("Quite the little noble savage!" one of his admirers exclaims), beyond his narrative function as an agent of the film's pervasive criticism of civilization's obtuseness and insensitivity, Kaspar comes to embody the primitive capacity for unimpeded vision that Herzog equates with the filmmaker's loftiest aspiration.

The mystery of Leonard Zelig is ultimately resolved: he is restored to health, happiness, and society through the love of a good woman. His only regret at the end of his life, the closing title tells us, is never having finished *Moby Dick*. The mystery of Kaspar Hauser remains inexpressible, at least in words, as the Rittmeister's scribe ironically confirms in the film's closing line when he celebrates the autopsy results revealing the murdered man's enlarged liver and unusual brain: "Finally we have an explanation for this strange man, and we cannot find a better one." Through his casting of Bruno S. in the title role and his expressionistic renderings of Kaspar's gnostic dreams, however, Herzog discovers cinematic alternatives to logocentric writing for reaffirming the mystery of Kaspar Hauser.

The life of the actor Bruno S. closely parallels that of the character he portrays: an apparently retarded street person of unknown origin, he first came to Herzog's attention after appearing in a documentary about mental institutions. His awkward body movements, untrained voice, and above all, preternatural gaze together create a nearly mystical, and to my knowledge, unprecedented film performance (fig. 19).[27] Of all the spies and ciphers of the cinema, his character alone seems unfathomable. "Who *was* this Leonard Zelig?" Why, Woody Allen, of course, the film's *auteur*. Who is this Chauncey Gardiner? Peter Sellers, an actor already famous for his disguises and multiple roles. To claim that Kaspar Hauser is Bruno S., however, is to express a tautology. The very antithesis of a movie star, Bruno remains as inaccessible and yet as "real" (a fact of nature) as the protagonist he portrays, his vision seemingly fixed on that "primordial *elsewhere*" Metz has defined as the space from which all cinematic signification originates.

Herzog represents this lost world through Kaspar's dream visions: the Caucasus, the procession up the mountain towards Death, the desert caravan. Employing formal techniques that draw attention to the specifically cinematic aspects of these exotic

FIGURE 19. *The Mystery of Kaspar Hauser*

sequences—slow motion, non-diegetic music, overexposed, monochromatic, or flattened images, and, most striking, flickering shadows—the director seeks out equivalences for his protagonist's unique, innocent perceptions, "the rough filmstock correlating to Kaspar's primal imagination" (Corrigan 139). Balanced by the equally stylized, symmetrically composed long takes of the landscape and the village as in the film's closing shot, these romantic visions critique the scribe's busy note-taking and complacent final pronouncement. The inadequacy of writing to resolve fundamental mysteries ("Hauser can tell you exactly what I look like and where I come from. To save you the trouble I'll tell you myself where I come from and even what my name is. M. L. O." reads the message left on Kaspar's body by his unidentified guardian-turned-murderer) provides not only the inspiration for Herzog's brand of expressionistic filmmaking but a cautionary reminder of the limitations inherent in every effort to define the phantom of the cinema.

CHAPTER SIX

◆

Documenting Character in
The Thin Blue Line

I wanted to make a film about self-deception . . . about
how our need to believe what we want to believe is a lot
stronger than our need to seek the truth.

—Errol Morris

Following a tradition established by Méliès's manipulation of the
screen image, numerous fiction features since *Citizen Kane* have
employed doctored newsreel footage with the paradoxical effect of
enhancing the film's verisimilitude while simultaneously demon-
strating how the camera is able to lie. In *Zelig*, for example, Woody
Allen's appearances amidst the celebrities of the 1920s serve mainly
to delight the spectator in the manner of Méliès's original cinema of
attractions; in the case of *In the Line of Fire*, Clint Eastwood's holo-
graphic image in the background of news footage centering on President Kennedy adds historical resonance as well as psychological credibility to the film's formulaic plot while also eliminating the less
satisfactory re-creations and impersonations used in earlier movies
like *The Day of the Jackal*. Indeed, the success of digitalized images
in blockbusters like *Forrest Gump* (1994) and *The Mask* (1994) may
ultimately transform the way we think about an actor's performance
as well as subvert the description of character I have been advancing
here by eliminating the element of the actor's "presence" entirely.[28]

Such deliberate manipulation of "real life" images has been, until recently, conventionally excluded from the documentary film, which, since Grierson and Flaherty, has aspired to represent an objective argument about truth as it is found in the historical, natural world. Nonfiction films as diverse as *Night Mail* (1936), *Harvest of Shame* (1960), and *The Times of Harvey Milk* (1984) have employed archival footage, evidentiary interviews, and voiceover commentary to construct a narrative that uncovers an apparently unmediated truth laid bare by the filmmaker's disinterested observation. More recently, however, under the influence of deconstructionist and postmodernist theory's concerns with deceptive signifiers, historical amnesia, and distracting, empty spectacles, new modes of documentary practice have emerged that foreground the filmmaker's role in shaping the discourse. Linda Williams has identified Claude Lanzmann's *Shoah* (1985) and Errol Morris's *The Thin Blue Line* (1987) as prime examples of the postmodern documentary's response to "the trauma of an inaccessible past" by highlighting the work of production and incorporating "a new presence in the persona of the documentarian" (12). Bill Nichols distinguishes between these two texts based on the filmmaker's emphasis on historical reference as opposed to the properties of the text itself; thus, he defines *Shoah* as "interactive" and *The Thin Blue Line* as "reflexive" documentaries:

> If the historical world is a meeting place for the processes of social exchange and representation in the interactive mode, the representation of the historical world becomes, itself, the topic of cinematic meditation in the reflexive mode. Rather than hearing the filmmaker engage solely in an interactive (participatory, conversational, or interrogative) fashion with other social actors, we now see or hear the filmmaker also engage in metacommentary, speaking to us less about the historical world itself, as in the expository and poetic or interactive and diaristic modes, than about the process of representation itself. (Reality 56)

Instead of manipulating documentary images to enhance the credibility of the fiction as in *Zelig*, Morris utilizes stylized re-creations, formally composed interviews, asynchronous music, carefully designed lighting effects, slow motion, and other cinematic devices associated with the expressionist tradition to underscore the competing discourses at work in *The Thin Blue Line*'s search for historical truth. To convey a complex reality, in other words, he has created a hybrid text—a nonfiction film that relies on many of the techniques of fiction.

THE WRONG MAN

The argument of *The Thin Blue Line* centers on the "wrong man" theme made popular by many of Alfred Hitchcock's movies and later borrowed by investigative television programs like *60 Minutes*. It seems appropriate, then, that Morris initially came to Dallas County, Texas, in 1986 to make a documentary about Dr. James Grigson, the notorious psychiatrist whose expert testimony about convicted murderers facing sentencing had earned him the nickname "Dr. Death." In the course of interviewing dozens of death row inmates, however, Morris discovered he was after the wrong man once he became acquainted with Randall Dale Adams, a man convicted a decade earlier of the unprovoked shooting death of a Dallas police officer, Robert Wood. After studying the facts of the case and trial testimony, Morris (himself a former private detective) became convinced of Adams's innocence and decided to make a film that would reveal not only the injustice of Adams's predicament but the identity of the real killer, David Harris.

The resulting text, titled after a phrase district attorney Douglas Mulder used to describe for the Adams jury the heroic role of police in protecting the public from anarchy, extends the normal bounds of investigative journalism to raise haunting questions about the objectivity of American justice as well as the nebulous border that separates imagination from truth. By breaking the rules of both media reporting and cinéma vérité, Morris challenges viewers to look with open eyes at a "closed case" that becomes progressively strange and new. By treating a true-life, character-centered story in a self-consciously stylized, expressionistic way, he apparently fulfills his artistic commitment to expose the institutionalized self-deception that led to Adams's conviction and life sentence. Williams aptly concludes her analysis of *The Thin Blue Line* by noting its critique of postmodern representation that "inevitably succumbs to the depthlessness of the simulacrum, or that . . . gives up on truth to wallow in the undecidabilities of representation" (20). "Truth is difficult to know," Morris has said. "It is not impossible to know."

While the discourse of *The Thin Blue Line*, what Nichols has called the "voice" of documentary, clearly constructs the case for

Adams's innocence, it also introduces another, imperfectly repressed voice, one that qualifies the truth claims of the dominant discourse. This voice, which qualifies the dominant voice's authority (its claim to have uncovered the truth in the Adams case), corresponds to the signifying mechanism of the cinema itself and speaks to "our need to believe what we want to believe," our desire to participate in the imaginary order that every film constructs. As a reflexive documentary reminding us that it is, after all, "only a film"—a crafted narrative dependent on certain fundamental deceptions temporarily accepted as representing reality—*The Thin Blue Line* complicates both our sense of superiority to Texas justice and our conviction of Randall Adams's total innocence. At the same time the film acquits Adams of the murder and points to David Harris as the almost certain killer, it illustrates the limitations of all documentaries to record the truth, the whole truth, and nothing but the truth, thereby qualifying the dominant discourse's typing of the two principal characters as innocent victim and evil traducer.

While it exposes the miscarriage of justice and explains how it could happen, *The Thin Blue Line* employs reflexive strategies to imply certain parallels between the operation of the legal system and the interpretive activity of the film spectator, suggesting how both institutions privilege the desire for belief over the desire for truth. As the law enforcement officials in Dallas County desired to believe in Adams's guilt, the film's audience desires to believe in Adams's innocence. By repeatedly re-creating events of the fatal evening according to the conflicting testimony of several dubious witnesses (including Wood's patrol partner) and emphasizing the artifice of the representation through such irrelevant, expressionist, and reflexive images as the microscopic close-up of popcorn at a drive-in movie's concession stand, Morris deliberately destroys the "special indexical bond between image and historical event," transforming the status of what is seen into an imaginary event despite its basis in historical fact (Nichols, Reality 20). In the process, his documentary seems to confirm Metz's dictum that every film is a fiction film.

In order to comprehend any movie, Metz has argued, the spectator must first accept a lie (that the actor or scene is actually present) and then correct it by perceiving "the photographed object as absent, its photograph as present, and the presence of this absence as signifying" (Imaginary 57). Although all films are indeed dependent on both ocular deception (persistence of vision, flicker fusion) and the spectator's suspension of disbelief in the unreality of the image, in the case of documentary the viewer may feel less prepared to correct the lie by resorting to the reminder that "it's only a movie," especially in the case of *The Thin Blue Line* when an actual person's life is at stake beyond the parameters of the text. The dominant voice of this documentary, after all, forcefully demands freedom for Randall Adams. Had there been no *other* voice, however, the film would hardly have transcended its genre and merited the detailed consideration it has received as a post-modern questioning of any language's access to truth. By fore-grounding the staged, constructed, dissonant, and incomplete ele-ments of its discourse and by frustrating efforts to define with certainty the moral dimensions of its two central characters, *The Thin Blue Line* encourages the spectator's correction of its own inherent deceptiveness and ultimately resonates with what Paul Ricoeur calls a "surplus of meaning" that ranges beyond any author's control and that can never be fully recuperated by a struc-tural analysis (Andrew, "Phenomenology" 631).

STYLE AND DISCOURSE

Morris's film deliberately rejects what Nichols has defined as the two earlier styles in the evolution of documentary: direct address (exemplified by Grierson's work or, more blatantly, by the *March of Time* series) and cinéma vérité ("Voice" 17).[29] The first mode now seems limited by its authoritarian tone and the second by its lim-ited perspective. Thus, *The Thin Blue Line* avoids voiceover narra-tion or (until the very end) subtitled identifications and violates the cinéma vérité conventions by mounting the camera on a tripod, employing theatrical lighting effects, and creating stylized re-enact-ments far from the streets and courtrooms of Dallas County. Instead of following these two older documentary traditions, Mor-ris synthesizes the more recent formal strategies of participant interviews and reflexivity to assert an unsettling paradox: only through artifice, through foregrounding the filmmaker as the manipulator of illusions and the fabricator of meaning, can the complex truth be approached. The film's expressionistic style becomes readily apparent through the use of such obtrusive formal elements as extreme close-ups (of cigarettes, typescript, and pop-corn), carefully arranged interview settings (the same lens, the same distance from the camera, the same eye level), slow motion pho-tography (a pen bouncing on a desk, a flying milkshake), and, perhaps most strikingly, a haunting musical score by Philip Glass whose obsessive repetitions echo the narrative's visual design (Rafferty 76). Together, these elements contribute a sense of abstraction to the discourse that seems at odds with the "true crime" nature of the story. Unlike a legal brief, where the facts of the argument speak for themselves and appeal to a logical reconstruction of events, *The Thin Blue Line* consistently employs subjective images and dissonant juxtapositions to remind viewers of the very ruptures in the text that all lawyers and most classical filmmakers seek to efface.

One particularly arresting moment early in the film may serve to illustrate the general effect of these devices. As an investigator recalls how the police eyewitness to the shooting (Teresa Turko) was hypnotized to try to help her recall the license plate of the killer's stolen car, Morris cuts to close-ups of a swinging pocket watch against a stark black background. Adding slow motion and an amplified swishing sound as the watch moves in and out of the frame, accompanied by the pronounced musical score, the film privileges the imaginary order induced by the flow of aural and visual sensations over the symbolic order represented by the off-screen narration of the lawman. The dangerous implications of this artfully created state of altered consciousness become immediately apparent: Morris concludes the sequence with a montage of zoom shots of the tailgates of several blue compact cars, each with a different license plate and slightly different light configuration (but all with the same red bumper sticker). These shots succeed one another too quickly for the spectator to make a positive identification. Soon after, the investigator admits that the police had been searching for the wrong car, a blue Comet instead of a blue Vega. The search in the earlier sequence has been undermined: unable initially to distinguish among the various blue images shown in the rapid zooms, the spectator now realizes that he or she also had been looking for the wrong referent signified by those partial, phantom images. Throughout the remainder of the film, eyewitnesses within the diegesis and audiences in front of the screen will be subject to the same misleading, sometimes willfully deceptive perceptions. The voice that asserts Adams's innocence remains mediated by the filmmaker's craft, allowing for other possible meanings. Thus, although Morris firmly believes that David Harris shot the policeman while sitting alone behind the wheel of a stolen car, his re-enactments depict the *witnesses'* accounts of two persons in the front seat and a bushy-haired gunman who resembles Adams at the

time, not Harris. In order to share the dominant discourse's conclusion about the crime, in other words, the viewer must see
through the images presented to the absent truth; once apprehended, that same truth—Adams is innocent, Harris is guilty—
becomes subtly qualified by other discordant or incomplete data
summoned forth by the text.

One way Morris introduces disharmony is through color. In
the opening title, for example, only the word "Blue" appears not in
white but in red, all four words intersected by a thin blue line,
introducing a paradigmatic image of cognitive dissonance. Two signifiers—language and color—conflict, leaving viewers confused
about not only what they have seen but about what is the "truth":
is that third word really red or really blue? In the diegesis, Morris
reveals that even red may not really be red by including an otherwise digressive portion of an interview with Judge Metcalfe in
which he describes how his father, an FBI officer, participated in the
capture of John Dillinger. The famous "Lady in Red" who lured
Dillinger to the Biograph Theatre that night, he tells us, was actually dressed in *orange*. This piece of "trivia," as Metcalfe calls it, is
visually re-created over his off-screen narration through old black-
and-white (fictional) footage in which the color of the woman's
dress can only be imagined.

Another example of color as a deceptive signifier occurs in the
interview with the prosecution's star witness, Mrs. Emily Miller.
She is first depicted in a courtroom artist's watercolor as a brunette,
which immediately conflicts with her actual appearance before the
camera as a bleached blonde and with later newspaper images of her
again with dark hair. This inconsistency—and the obvious artificiality of her present appearance (reinforced by cuts during the
interview to scenes from her favorite old movie, *Boston Blackie*)—
underscores her status as a false witness but also leaves the question of her true hair color (brown? blonde? gray?) unresolved, permanently absent from the text.

Morris uses images of incompleteness as well as dissonance to
establish specular uncertainty. For example, at the first mention of
the "break" in the case, a report of a stolen car from Vidor, Texas,
home of David Harris, the film cuts to an extreme close-up of a road
map with Vidor at the center. Without the larger map of Texas or
some proximate familiar cities such as Dallas or Houston, most
viewers will remain confused about Vidor's location. In a parallel
piece of editing, when Metcalfe mentions that Dillinger's moll,
"the Lady in Red," was subsequently deported to Eastern Europe,

Morris cuts to a map of Czechoslovakia. In both cases, the discourse seems to stray from the essential argument and to suggest that the film's quest for truth cannot be guided by any clear map. Similarly, numerous close-ups of newspaper items related to the case isolate a single word or phrase without providing sufficient explanatory context, offering only a pastiche of images without depth or reference. More fundamental to the structure of the discourse, the omission of identifying subtitles for interviewees or voiceover to cover temporal transitions forces the audience to revert, at least temporarily, from the symbolic order of language conventionally prioritized by expository documentaries to the imaginary, constructing a presence from absence (e.g., "This must be the trial judge"). This process of comprehending characters by correcting the "lie" built into the cinema's process of signification ultimately involves overturning the judicial process that convicted Randall Adams.

THE PHANTOM OF CHARACTER

The Adams trial hinged on the issue of identification, beginning with the confusion of the blue Comet for the Vega and ending with the dubious testimony of witnesses who placed Adams at the crime scene. *The Thin Blue Line* hinges on the issue of character, the filmed testimony of Adams and Harris about their activities on the night of the shooting. As the "wrong man" theme unfolds and Adams emerges as a victim of injustice, the spectator's attention shifts to broader questions of personal character, a process that confounds our certainty of Adams's innocence and Harris's guilt. The film confuses even the initial recognition of Adams, who first appears clean shaven with light brown hair cut short immediately after the image of a newspaper photograph depicting a bushy-haired man with a droopy mustache being arrested in Dallas. In his review of *The Thin Blue Line*, Terrence Rafferty notes the spectral quality of Adams's appearance: "a wan, ghostly, soft-spoken man . . .—he looks and sounds like someone on the verge of disappearing" (77). This description evokes the ghostly memory of another drifter accused of a confounding murder in Dallas, Lee Harvey Oswald.[30] Because Adams is dressed in a plain white shirt in an apparently comfortable setting, the spectator who is led by the editing and the speaker's opening words ("The day they picked me up . . .") to identify this man as the accused may remain uncertain about his present status as a convicted murderer. The question of his credibility is immediately raised by a cut to the homicide detective on the case, Gus Rose, who tells the unseen interviewer that he could tell immediately that the suspect "didn't have much of a conscience" when he was interrogated. "He had done other things that he told me about that didn't seem to bother him in the least." These "other things" remain unspecified throughout *The Thin Blue Line*—the phrase itself unmentioned in reviews and articles about the film— and seem irrelevant to the dominant voice that pronounces Adams's innocence of the crime, but they linger in the viewer's mind, speaking about the incomprehensible nature of Adams's moral character, which, like all human identities, must remain ungraspable to the last.

The film constructs the character of Randall Adams in a way that ultimately undermines every effort to know him. Just as Gus Rose labels him conscienceless after first meeting him, Dr. Grigson testifies at the trial that he is a Hitler, a Charlie Manson, someone who could "work all day and creep all night." Adams's demeanor and articulateness before the camera belie these descriptions (the reviewer for *The Nation*, Fredric Paul Smoles, credits him with "remarkable dignity; he is an eerily calm man with flashes of cool humor, and a manner that seems to register the injustice and inhumanity he has encountered with a kind of quiet amazement" [543]). Still, the spectator's approval must be qualified in two ways: the intrusion of "other things" within the diegesis and the awareness of the filmmaker's manipulative control. Even when Adams discusses his signed statement early in the film, his speech patterns seem mannered and his words carefully chosen. While denying that it was an actual confession, as the police and newspapers later described it, Adams recounts revising the text and never asserts that the final document recorded the unvarnished truth: "When it was basically what I liked, yes, I signed it." The film's presentation of the crucial document compounds the equivocation. Morris cuts into Adams's narration with partial shots of trivial details like the time and date, extreme close-ups of key phrases ("I do not remember"), and full shots of the typescript in which the words cannot be read. The sequence consists almost entirely of language—voiceover combined with printed words—but the discourses they enunciate remain incomplete and inconclusive, a fragmented version of the truth.

Two other diegetic elements disturb the discourse proclaiming Adams's innocence. The first is the missing testimony of

Adams's brother, his alibi for the hours of the crime. This critical witness, never named within the film, failed to appear at the trial or in front of Morris's camera, being represented instead only by a snapshot. His absence leaves an inexplicable gap in the otherwise nearly seamless defense.[31] But the most disruptive moments of the repressed discourse come when Adams himself describes the sequence of events that brought him together with David Harris, who had picked him up after his car had run out of gas. What was Adams doing driving around with a sixteen-year-old who displayed an "arsenal" in the trunk, shot a pistol out the car window, and smoked marijuana all evening? And why did he first agree to go to a drive-in movie with Harris, then rather prudishly insist on leaving during the second soft core picture ("I didn't really care for the second feature, which is an R-rated cheerleader type thing")? As with the Dillinger and *Boston Blackie* sequences, Morris punctuates Adams's narration with brief scenes from the two low-budget movies playing that night, *Student Body* and *Swinging Cheerleaders*, to remind viewers of the interplay between fictional and real in every cinematic experience. The latent homosexuality suggested by Adams's behavior (neither confirmed nor denied by other details in the film) cannot be entirely dismissed by the spectator convinced of his innocence in the murder case but aware of the mixed motives that make us all something less than "straight."[32]

The gaps in Adams's narration, the cinematic representation of his official statement, and the numerous reconstructions of the crime produce both a "surplus of meaning" and the "psychological discomfort" that Leon Festinger defines as the consequence of cognitive dissonance (2). On the one hand, the spectator recognizes that Adams and the others are not actors in the usual sense (Nichols uses the term "social actor" to define how observed individuals in nonfiction films represent themselves to others); on the other hand, he or she realizes that the interviews have been rehearsed and edited, not unlike the prosecuting attorney's tactic of "coaching the witness" that David Harris describes. Similarly, though the story has been determined by historical events, the plot has been organized by a dominant discourse. By foregrounding the expressionistic elements of that discourse while at the same time eliminating the actual voice or on-screen presence of the subjective narrator identifying characters and controlling signifiers, however, *The Thin Blue Line* avoids the ideological narrowness of vérité films like *Harlan County, U.S.A.* (1976), interview compilations like *The Life and Times of Rosie the Riveter* (1980), and interactive documentaries like *Roger and Me* (1989). Few nonfiction films, in fact, so purpose-fully explore the tension between artifice and objectivity, between the imaginary and the real, and between guilt and innocence.

In "correcting the lie" that sentenced Randall Adams to life imprisonment, the film presents a powerful case against David Har-ris. In many ways, however, it constructs his character as a kind of double of Adams. His very words in describing the crucial events ("The story I told was . . .") echo the equivocal nature of Adams's offi-cial statement; his placement slightly angled against a dark back-ground in the right center of the frame duplicates Adams's interview position; his Vidor friend's description of him as having no con-science repeats precisely Gus Rose's depiction of Adams; he too has been convicted of (a different) murder and is now serving a life sen-tence (figs. 20, 21). These parallels may remind viewers that Harris is the same age at the time of filming as Adams was at the time of the crime. They suggest the thin line that separates one man's fate, and perhaps one man's character, from another. By alternating their con-flicting narrations and yet affirming their connection to a single fatal event (the murder of Officer Wood, now recuperated by *The Thin Blue Line*), the film enunciates both a dialectic and a synthesis. Its dominant voice—articulated through the diegesis—is dialectical: Adams is essentially telling the truth; Harris has lied. But its other voice—articulated primarily through the form—is synthetic: all truth is mediated; human character lies beyond knowing. Faulkner's aphorism about the novel applies equally to film: "how false the most profound book turns out to be when applied to life" (455).

Morris confirms the limits of his own approach to truth with a somewhat surprising resolution to the film's narrative structure. Rather than ending with the focus on Adams, he concludes by con-centrating on David Harris. In a disturbing coda to the public record of Harris's numerous violent crimes culminating in his murder conviction, Morris recovers a tempting clue from David's child-hood. His four-year-old brother (again, like Adams's brother, unnamed as well as absent except for a photograph) had drowned in a swimming pool accident when David was three. Over a montage of black-and-white photographs of the Harris family before and after the tragedy, David describes his brother's death and the dete-riorating relationship with his father that followed: " I guess that must have been some kind of traumatic experience for me." The sequence ends with a lengthy close-up of a snapshot of David at about age ten staring directly at the camera, his eyes masked by shadow (fig. 22). Like similar photographic images in fiction films—

FIGURE 20. *The Thin Blue Line*

FIGURE 21. *The Thin Blue Line*

the tracking shot towards the young girl's eye at the end of Polanski's *Repulsion* (1965), the close-up of the Warsaw ghetto child in Bergman's *Persona*, or the final freeze frame of the boy on the beach in Truffaut's *The 400 Blows* (1959)—this detail records the presence of an absence, a youth simultaneously lost and preserved, that also reflects the nature of cinema's imaginary signifier. When David Harris actually was present before *that* camera, Morris was absent; when Morris is present to interview him, *that* David Harris has been forever lost, leaving behind only the tracings represented by the photograph and the off-screen voice of his older, imprisoned self. The spectator is left to contemplate the portrait of a human face, which, especially in the cinema, seems to signify more than any verbal testimony.[33] The photograph of David as a child serves a similar function as the revelation of Rosebud at the end of *Citizen Kane*: a missing piece of the puzzle and not its solution, it signifies an irretrievable possibility that complicates rather than clarifies our comprehension of character. Just as Adams appears not entirely innocent, Harris must not be judged entirely guilty, but neither does the recovered clue exonerate him.

Like many postmodern works, *The Thin Blue Line* concludes on a note of indeterminacy—despite the truth it uncovers regarding Adams's non-involvement in the death of Officer Wood. The film's penultimate image is a close-up of an audio cassette recorder playing back what an intertitle identifies as the last interview with David Harris. Although the voices of Errol Morris and David Harris can be clearly heard, the dialogue appears subtitled over extreme close-ups of the tape machine (fig. 23). The formal presentation is reflexive in several ways: the narrative voice of this documentary is finally heard, the filmmaker himself acknowledging his role in constructing the discourse; the printed words similarly mark the authoritative text, allowing for no misunderstanding of the aural images; the image of the tape unwinding from its spool reflects the unseen process of the film unwinding from its reel—the entropic process bringing the text to its inevitable conclusion. For one last time, Morris inscribes the paradigm of presence of absence by replacing the human speakers—Harris and himself as actors—with a machine that records sound but not pictures. Neither of the voices we hear is embodied before the camera, nor are they speaking at the time the camera is operating. Remarkably, the exchange itself, which promises to be definitive ("On December 5, 1986, David Harris was interviewed one last time"), offers only the phantom of truth.

FIGURE 22. *The Thin Blue Line*

FIGURE 23. *The Thin Blue Line*

EM: Is he innocent?

DH: Did you ask him?

EM: Well, he's always said he's been innocent.

DH: There you go. Didn't believe him, huh? Criminals always lie.

EM: Well, what do you think . . . about whether he's innocent?

DH: I'm sure he is.

EM: How can you be sure?

DH: 'Cause I'm the one that knows.

For all the circumstantial evidence against Harris that precedes it, this interview leaves the spectator in much the same position as the Dallas investigators after interrogating their suspect, contemplating a blank, the equivalent of the typed "XXXXXX" that Morris closes in on at the bottom of Adams's official statement. How are we to resolve the cognitive dissonance conveyed in Harris's version of the Cretans paradox ("Criminals always lie")? The film's final image involves a quick cut to the swirling red police patrol light, a warning, perhaps, about the limited authority of both the law and the documentary filmmaker's art.

In an ironic postscript to the production of *The Thin Blue Line*, the definitive work of the justice system and the filmmaker has been further brought into question. Shortly after the movie's release in 1988, Randall Adams was released from prison after a new appeal overturned his conviction. Because Dallas County refused to retry him, however, he was never legally exonerated and has since written his own book (*Adams v. Texas* [New York: St. Martin's, 1991]) to establish his innocence. Since gaining his freedom, he has also instituted legal action against Errol Morris in an effort to share the profits from *The Thin Blue Line*.[34]

CHAPTER SEVEN

◆

Avatars of Memory:
Entropy and Nostalgia in the
Representation of Character

Some people just got faces that stick in your mind.

—*On the Waterfront*

Film characters bear the burden of memory in various ways. Drawing on Barthes's definition of the "photo effect" and, presumably, Metz's explanation of the "lost object" status of the filmic signifier, John Ellis has summarized how "the irreducible separation that cinema maintains (and attempts to abolish) . . . can produce an almost intolerable nostalgia" (58–59). Because places rarely display such conspicuous signs of erosion from our earliest recollection of seeing them and because historical periods recreated in film have been directly experienced by relatively few, if any, contemporary viewers, the actor/character becomes the usual site of the spectator's nostalgia, as can be demonstrated most clearly in the typical response to watching home movies, reminiscing over "the way *we* were." Similarly, when we view the televised image of a bloated Marlon Brando rambling incoherently and slobbering on the embarrassed host of *Larry King Live*, we may simultaneously recall the virile energy of the young man whose powerful yet graceful appearance in *On the Waterfront* commands the memory of everyone he

119

encounters. "I remembered you the first moment I saw you," Edie tells Terry as they walk in the park; "When you weighed 168 pounds you were beautiful," his brother Charlie reminds him in the taxi. As Edie's recollection attempts to bridge the gap that now separates them, Charlie's comment acknowledges the difference between then and now. Watching *On the Waterfront* then (in 1954), the film spectator remains aware of not only how the middleweight who fought Wilson that night has been transformed into a "bum" but of how the actor impersonating him will also inevitably be lost, absorbed into other roles. Watching it now (as with watching *Citizen Kane*), the same spectator may comprehend more deeply how the expanse of history has modified—with ironic and possibly tragic implications—the actor's image.

Woody Allen invokes this sense of imminent loss, what might be termed "premature nostalgia," in the closing scene of *Manhattan* (1979) when his character implores the eighteen-year-old Tracy (Mariel Hemingway) not to accept a scholarship to study dramatic arts in London. Having discovered that "Tracy's face" belongs on a short list of "Things That Make Life Worth Living," Isaac reverses his former argument and tries to convince her not to be seduced by the actor's life: "I just don't want that thing I like about you to change." The poignancy of his plea is immediately compounded by Tracy's somewhat self-contradictory reply: "Everybody gets corrupted. You have to have a little faith in people."[35] The lingering close-ups of Hemingway's youthful face at this moment convey, by prolepsis rather than mimesis, something of the same romantic melancholy to be found in the mirror shot of Catherine at her dressing table in *Jules and Jim*. For all of Hemingway's unspoiled beauty in her first leading role, the viewer senses the hopeless dream of the lover (Isaac)/director (Allen)'s idealization of her as well as the painful truth of the aspiring (Tracy)/fledgling (Hemingway) actress' acknowledgment of mutability. The proof of Tracy's bittersweet comment about corruption already existed for the film's original audience in the disastrously brief movie career of Mariel's older sister, Margot Hemingway; for viewers now, it lies in Margot's premature death as well as the twisted history of Mariel's own disappointing roles and personal transformations (including, most notoriously, the breast implants she received before appearing in *Star 80* [1983], a movie about the exploitation and murder of a naive young actress).[36]

The narrative of *Manhattan* concludes on a note of indeterminacy befitting, I would argue, the phantom quality of Tracy's character. As she mulls over his last-minute plea, Allen employs a close-up of Isaac awaiting her response, resisting her call for patience and trust and hopefully gazing at her face for a sign of his success. Tracy never does decide what to do; instead, Allen cuts to the panoramic skyline of Manhattan as the sound track takes up Gershwin's "Rhapsody in Blue." Immortalized by the camera, poised between New York and London, childhood and adulthood ("I turned eighteen the other day," she tells Isaac, "I'm legal, but I'm still a kid") in a primordial elsewhere and elsewhen, she becomes at the instant of this unexpected cut another phantom of the cinema in the special sense I have been using the term. Unlike the other characters in the film, whose "irreducible separation" from the spectator has been effaced through conventional means, Tracy remains, like "God's answer to Job" as Isaac had earlier described her, the uncanny sign of an inaccessible presence. The orchestral music and lush images that comprise *Manhattan's* extradiegetic coda serve to compensate for her absence, the swelling theme and spectacular black-and-white cityscapes vividly recalling the grandeur of an era already perceived as past. This ending corresponds to Fredric Jameson's description of the "nostalgia film," offering "a perception of the present as history; that is, as a relationship to the present which somehow defamiliarizes it and allows us that distance which is at length characterized as a historical perspective" (284). Rather than seeking to recover a vanished past through period detail or homage to *auteurs* and genres, the films to be discussed in this chapter embody nostalgia in their phantom protagonists, avatars of memory who simultaneously signify their own history and transcend their own extinction.

THE LAST TYCOON

The protagonist of F. Scott Fitzgerald's unfinished novel and Elia Kazan's last film, Monroe Stahr, offers a unique example of the "irreducible separation" personified by the phantom of the cinema. As initially conceived by Fitzgerald (clearly based on his acquaintance with Irving Thalberg), brought to the screen by Kazan, screenwriter Harold Pinter, and producer Sam Spiegel, and performed by Robert DeNiro, Stahr incarnates the imaginative lives of at least half a dozen *auteurs*, revealing at once the unfulfilled promise of the "boy wonders" Fitzgerald and Thalberg, the idealized alter egos of the aging Kazan and Spiegel, and the expressive muteness of Pinter and (in this role) DeNiro. As a result, *The Last Tycoon* (1976) is reflexive in the conventional sense of explicitly representing the processes of film production but also in the sense of reifying the elusiveness, indeterminacy, and evanescence of the cinema's particular mode of representation. As the adaptation of an unfinished manuscript about an era in Hollywood irrevocably lost between the time of the novel's conception and the film's own construction, *The Last Tycoon*, unlike its contemporaries, *The Day of the Locust* (1975), *Hearts of the West* (1975), *W. C. Fields and Me* (1976),and *Gable and Lombard* (1976), seeks to restore not simply the golden days of Hollywood but the haunting spirit of the cinema itself.

Of course, all adaptations of previously published material, particularly those derived from the works of canonical authors like Fitzgerald, must negotiate between the claims of the original literary text and the need to function as independent narratives in a different medium. While *The Last Tycoon* appears to be generally "faithful" to Fitzgerald's manuscript as edited by Edmund Wilson and posthumously published in 1941—slavishly so in the opinion of Pauline Kael, who criticized Kazan's decision not to revise Pinter's script as misguided "reverence piled upon reverence" (159–60)—the film does incorporate some important changes. The novel's opening episode at the Hermitage in Nashville is discarded in favor of parallel scenes taking place at the studio; Cecilia Brady's importance is considerably reduced by eliminating her role as narrator; her father's character retains little trace of the treachery Fitzgerald intended to develop; Kathleen Moore's impoverished background and flirtatious behavior are similarly deleted. All of these simplifications tend to concentrate narrative attention on the character of Monroe Stahr. The one major expansion from the novel, in fact, may be more significant than all that is missing since it reverberates throughout the rest of the film. This is the scene in the producer's office—three inches of type preserved intact for about three minutes of screen time—where Stahr describes to Boxley, the studio's imported "prestige" writer, the art of "making pictures." Boxley has been summoned to revise an incompetent script he had submitted. After exposing the British novelist's condescending attitude towards the movies, Stahr offers the following practical lesson in screenwriting:

> "Suppose you're in your office. You've been fighting duels or writing all day and you're too tired to write any more. You're sitting there staring—dull, like we all get sometimes. A pretty

stenographer that you've seen before comes into the room and you watch her—idly. She doesn't see you, though you're very close to her. She takes off her gloves, opens her purse and dumps it out on a table—"

Stahr stood up, tossing his key ring on his desk.

"She has two dimes and a nickel—and a cardboard match box. She leaves the nickel on the desk, puts the two dimes back into her purse and takes her black gloves to the stove, opens it and puts them inside. There is one match in the match box and she starts to light it kneeling by the stove. You notice that there's a stiff wind blowing in the window—but just then your telephone rings. The girl picks it up, says hello—listens—and says deliberately into the phone, 'I've never owned a pair of black gloves in my life.' She hangs up, kneels by the stove again, and just as she lights the match, you glance around very suddenly and see that there's another man in the office, watching every move the girl makes—"

Stahr paused. He picked up his keys and put them in his pocket.

"Go on," said Boxley smiling. "What happens?"

"I don't know," said Stahr. "I was just making pictures."
(42–43)

DeNiro and Donald Pleasence combine to make this set piece a tour de force, the heretofore phlegmatic Stahr moving about the room as if playing an animated game of charades, the previously diffident Boxley his enraptured audience. Until this moment, DeNiro has underplayed the role, informing his character with a stolidity that signifies Stahr's lingering grief over the death of his wife and the chronic illness threatening his own life; now the actor seems possessed by the ghost of the hyperactive Johnny-boy, his signature performance in *Mean Streets* (1973). At last, perhaps a third of the way through the film, Stahr's creative energy has been *presented*, eliminating the necessity for the novel's lengthy story conference and several other descriptive passages from Cecilia's point of view.

The Boxley episode thus confirms Stahr's talent for moviemaking, his ability to generate a spontaneous illusion and to convince a sophisticated viewer of its reality. Like Fitzgerald's earlier character, Jay Gatsby, Stahr has embodied a "heightened sensitivity to the promises of life" by inventing his own "vital illusion" (Gatsby 2)—not merely the scenario he has just brought to life but the ghostly figure of Kathleen Moore, whom he has constructed as the avatar of his deceased wife, the movie star Minna Davis. In this sudden flash of illumination staged for Boxley's benefit, he has fulfilled Tolstoy's prophecy for"the little clicking contraption" that was to transform the life of writers. But this inspired moment also marks the apogee of Stahr's art and the beginning of the film's long, entropic denouement. As *The Last Tycoon* unwinds, the spectator witnesses the gradual exhaustion of Stahr's gift as his lightning genius dims into silence and darkness.

The significance of the Boxley episode is reinforced by two later scenes: first, when Stahr invents a story to placate Cecilia Brady about meeting an old friend at the Writer's Ball and driving him around Hollywood, and later in his moments alone after being told of his enforced "vacation" when he imagines Kathleen Moore, now married, re-enacting the tale he had created for Boxley. Both sequences take place in his office, the site of the original Boxley interview. In the first, his deception serves no higher purpose than to avoid a confrontation with the lovesick producer's daughter over his actually leaving the dance with Kathleen. This time, however, his invention proves far less successful than it had with Boxley. Rather than being taken in by the story, Cecilia merely goes along with it, quietly weeping as the tale concludes. DeNiro suggests something compulsive and pathetic in Stahr's contrived embellishments, climaxed by his sentimental sigh over the memory of the entirely fictional "old Gus"—an addition in the film to the episode as Fitzgerald wrote it.

Stahr's false nostalgia turns to genuine grief when he repeats the Boxley story for himself with Kathleen now playing the role of the mysterious girl. Looking directly at the camera this time, alone in his office, Stahr recites the monologue while the film cuts to shots of Kathleen burning letters in a fireplace as her husband watches. When he concludes again, "I don't know, I was just making pictures," he directly addresses the audience. The camera then cuts from Stahr to a matching close-up of Kathleen, her eyes, like Cecilia's before, filled with tears. In the scene's final cut back to Stahr he appears shrunken even in close-up as a voiceover echoes his parting words to Kathleen: "I don't want to lose you." This scene crystallizes the inertia that has engulfed both Stahr and the film itself as it winds down to its muted conclusion. Stahr's repeated phrase about "just making pictures" elicits the memory of the earlier, energized moment when he had beguiled Boxley, the spectator's surrogate, but it also forces the acknowledgment that like Gatsby, Stahr has dreamed only of reliving the past, imagining in Kathleen Moore the phantom double of his departed wife. Although the film preserves Fitzgerald's admiration for both men's romantic capacity for dreaming, it also confirms his tragic awareness of how the object of the dream, once obtained, tends to lose its enchantment. Thus Stahr's pursuit of Kathleen (like Gatsby's of Daisy Buchanan) deteriorates into a series of empty gestures and diminished options. Here, the cross-cutting combined with the juxtaposition of voiceover with the depiction of action and space beyond his knowledge or control reduces his former power of invention to mere repetition.

The poignancy of Stahr's lost dream is matched by the film's elegiac evocation of the aesthetic dreams once realized by certain powerful Hollywood movies. Thus, *The Last Tycoon* begins in the studio screening room with Stahr offering commentary on the dailies from three pictures in production: a black-and-white gangster film, a Technicolor romance, and another black-and-white melodrama. Together, they constitute virtually the Argument for the film to follow:

1. A *femme fatale* meets her gangster boyfriend in an Italian restaurant; as she leaves for the powder room, he is executed by machine gun fire from a passing car.
2. A young woman walks away from her lover on an empty beach; the camera stays on his reaction.
3. A foreign woman and her Latin lover conduct an affair in her apartment; after her husband phones, she tells her lover to leave, then changes her mind and tells him to stay.

The first sequence foreshadows Stahr's ultimate destruction, which is linked both to a woman's betrayal and the forces of unseen, nefarious men (collectively referred to as "New York" in the film). The second anticipates his love affair with Kathleen at the unfinished beach house he is building and her eventual departure from his life. The third specifically refers to Kathleen in several ways: she is British, her "nos" to Stahr repeatedly turn out to mean "yes," and she belongs to another man who is always absent.

When examined closely, each of these movie clips reveals the presence of absence paradigm that I have invoked to relate the construction of character to self-reflexivity. In the gangster film, the fatal action is precipitated by the woman's departure from the frame, her absence signalling the moment of execution.[37] In the beach sequence, Stahr draws attention to the woman's absence by specifically criticizing the editing, demanding that the camera follow the girl because "She's the one we're interested in." In the melodrama, the presence of the absent husband is confirmed by his phone call, which, like the phone call in the Boxley episode, again precipitates the significant action, the wife's change of heart.

A subsequent scene from this last movie—the only one whose progress is followed through production—involves intertextuality as well as entropy. The adulterous woman played by a talented prima donna named Didi (Jeanne Moreau) sings a farewell to her lover, the cabaret owner played by Rodriguez (Tony Curtis), before rejoining her husband. The plot clearly foreshadows Kathleen's decision to marry another man instead of staying with Stahr; the song itself, "You Had Your Chance," echoes in the very next sequence when Stahr cannot bring himself to ask Kathleen to stay with him when he sees her for the last time. The entire scene has been horridly written by Boxley, who has already been fired and is now absent from the screening room, but whose presence is continually felt in the absurd dialogue that Stahr disgustedly calls his "going away present." Stahr is thus left to preside over a "prestige picture" that obviously represents a *Casablanca*-in-the-making (an odd allusion, simultaneously anticipating the 1942 classic within the larger film's diegetic time—mid 1930s—and imitating it from the present): the wife in trench coat, the underground cafe, the soulful piano accompaniment, the lover's toast—"Here's to you, kid." Rodriguez is clearly a stand-in for Bogart, Didi for Ingrid Bergman (both actors, in another sense, avatars of their own younger selves). At the same time the references make the imaginary movie recognizable and "real," the parodic elements suggest the withdrawal of the delegated images on the screen by referring us to an "original," superior filmic text, *Casablanca*, of which the present representation is a de-energized, degraded, and ultimately doomed version. Stahr can intervene, as he did earlier on the set by removing the director, to bring about the picture's completion, but he cannot by rewriting or reshooting bring it to life.

The conclusion of *The Last Tycoon*—a scene that is entirely Kazan's invention—has been criticized for being evasive, but perhaps its open-endedness can be understood as an appropriate analogue for the aura of possibility left behind by Fitzgerald's unfinished manuscript. Earlier in the film, the image of the half-constructed beach house had served as a vivid symbol of Stahr's unfulfilled ambitions, the skeleton, as it were, of his own private Xanadu. The film's final vision, a long shot of Stahr walk-

ing into a dark and empty sound stage, conjures up the nostalgia
and decay associated with the last days of the old Hollywood.
Leonard and Barbara Quart have defined this concluding view of
Stahr and, as it has turned out, the final image in the cinema of Elia
Kazan:[38] "All light goes out, it suggests not only Stahr's death and
the novel's blackout with Fitzgerald's death, but also Stahr dissolv-
ing finally into the maw of picture-making, as more prosaic men
merely go back into the earth" (46). Like the concluding long shot
in *On the Waterfront* it resembles, one that suggests in retrospect
how Terry may be less liberated than trapped when he passes under
the iron door and enters the huge shed, this image of Stahr has a
double edge. An elegiac tribute to a bygone era of movie-making, it
also immortalizes Stahr through the very act of his recession into
darkness. He does not die on screen, he is not destroyed by "New
York," but instead removes himself to a place *elsewhere*, beyond
the vanishing point, to live on as the phantom of the cinema. As
Kathleen has proven to be the lost object, the distant star, of his
vital illusion, so he himself has become the Stahr of the spectator's
own perception.

Fitzgerald wrote a passage in *The Last Tycoon* that speaks to
the special process by which such elusive film characters can be
apprehended. "You can take Hollywood for granted like I did, or
you can dismiss it with the contempt we reserve for what we don't
understand. It can be understood too, but only dimly and in
flashes" (10). In the static darkness of the screening room or the
empty sound stage, in the lightning brilliance of the Boxley episode,
Stahr has embodied the character of narrative cinema, its dialectical impulse for creativity and entropy.

THREE FRENCH FILMS

As conceived by Fitzgerald and realized by Kazan (the French word
for director is *"réalisateur"*), Stahr represents an ego ideal, one who
proves capable—for a time—of succeeding within the Hollywood
system without compromising his artistic integrity. The nostalgia
the film elicits ultimately has less to do with Jameson's description
of postmodernism's "desperate attempt to appropriate a missing
past" (19) than with the desire to recover what Conrad once defined
as the artless self's secret sharer, "that ideal conception of one's
own personality every man sets up for himself" (Sharer 138). Like
the remaining films to be discussed in this chapter, then, *The Last*

Tycoon remains primarily a work of high modernism, mixing memory and desire (to borrow Eliot's phrase) while retaining some sense of "being," no matter how elusive. The nostalgic memory personified in these works is that of a unified, uncorrupted, and unassailable selfhood whose implacable enemy becomes the very process of history. In such films as *Jules and Jim*, Louis Malle's *Lacombe, Lucien* (1974), and Bertrand Tavernier's *Daddy Nostalgia* (1990), characters enact the unwinding of their own material existence through the projector: they simply run out of time.

We have already suggested in chapter one how the close-up of Moreau's reflection in the dressing mirror in *Jules and Jim* prompts our yearning for an image of beauty at once present and fading before us. Several other dramatic moments within the film seek to preserve the ideal vision Catherine has incarnated for the men who worship her against the entropic forces of her own biology and the destructive whirlwind of European history. In each case, Truffaut employs the stylistic resources of New Wave cinema in the paradoxical cause of affirming her significance as an ideal and acknowledging her human vulnerability. Beginning with the montage of close-ups that accompany her initial appearance and that repeat the dramatic series of zooms, pans, and tracking shots circling around the stone figure she is thought to resemble, these formal flourishes link the film's reflexive inquiry into the nature of art with the mythic dimensions of Catherine's character.

Like the cinema, Catherine is a hybrid, the offspring of well-born (artistic) and plebeian (commercial) impulses living halfway between the spiritual realm the men associate with high art (translating literature, purchasing Picassos) and the mundane world of popular culture she struggles to accommodate (impersonating Chaplin's "Charlot" in the streets). As evanescent as the flickering images made alternately present and absent by the shutter mechanism, she speaks the film's very first words ("You said to me: I love you. I said to you: wait. I was going to say: take me. You said to me: go away."), emanating from the off-screen darkness, propelling the images into action, and describing the *fort/da* game that the cinema always plays and that this particular film now cogently represents through Moreau's disembodied, dislocated voice. As combustible as nitrate (her dress catches fire early on, her ashes are the subject of contestation at the end), she flirts and flees with equal force. She is also a male fantasy ("a queen . . . *une vraie femme*," Jules calls her), the unobtainable object of every man's—including Truffaut's—gaze. The moment her companions ignore her, she rebels—either playfully, as when she slaps Jules for not responding to her jokes, or more disturbingly, as when she leaps into the Seine in response to their disparaging remarks about women after attending a Strindberg play and, in the film's climax, when she drives off with Jim and commands Jules to watch. The freeze frames Truffaut employs on the first of these occasions identify her again with the statue the men had initially seen in slide projection; through the artifice of the cinema, they also capture her smile at its apex of influence and glory.

In spite of the men's efforts to tame her mercurial moods and the filmmaker's determination to preserve her mysterious seductiveness— "The gamble for me," Truffaut declared," was to make the woman moving (without being melodramatic) and not a tart" (qtd. in Bayer 159)—Catherine comes to represent decadence as well as timelessness. Certainly, she assumes nearly all the burden of aging in the film, her miscarriage marking a watershed in the representation of her character in the same way the war marks an end to *la belle époque.* As the vitality of the film's style throughout the first third of the narrative—exemplified by the rapid cutting, the moving camera sometimes mounted on bicycles or soaring high above the countryside, the panning shots creating tapestries of bohemian Paris—gives way to the more somber and static scenes of the last third, the ideal of friendship and love created by the trio can only be sustained by the spectator's memory of what they—and especially Catherine—once seemed to be. While she becomes, like the weathered statue projected by Albert's magic lantern immediately before the stone figure the men come to worship, "*très pathétique,*" neurotic, tyrannical, perhaps morally insane, she is also the victim of biology (being older than Jim and unable to bear his children), patriarchy (protesting Strindberg's and Baudelaire's misogyny, which the men complacently admire), and history.

When the men meet for the last time at the Cinema des Ursulines (a favorite haunt of the New Wave group), they lament the Nazi book burnings that signify not only the destruction of the culture they have helped to create and fought to preserve but also their ultimate inadequacy as artists to sustain their own vital illusions, inspired by and embodied in Catherine. Cavell has noted how the newsreel of the bonfire differs from the earlier documentary footage depicting Parisian scenes and then the Great War:

Truffaut uses the nostalgia of the old photographs of Paris streets and houses, and the heartbreaking beauty and terror of

the soldiers rising like flowers from their fields, to open us to
the knowledge that these mortals whose lives we have been
shown and will be shown were there in the only world we
inhabit. . . . The clip of the book-burning reinforces this meaning by showing us an event taking place at a time the men are
not there. It therewith serves to rebuke their absence, or to
state that the world has passed them by. (141)

Perhaps it is because Catherine acknowledges this failure, or perhaps because she alone has remained an unregenerate noncon-
formist, true to the iconoclastic, spontaneous spirit that had once
bound them together, that she decides to save what she can by
destroying the triangle, thereby memorializing the community
they had once been.

Lacombe, Lucien takes up the theme of European history a
decade after *Jules and Jim* concludes. The narrative is set in south-
western France during the summer of 1944; it tells the story of a
rather sullen, bored peasant boy named Lucien Lacombe (Pierre
Blaise) who drifts into working for the German police after being
casually turned down by the local resistance leader. While carrying
out his routinely cruel duties for the Gestapo, he becomes involved
with the once distinguished family of a Jewish tailor from Paris,
Albert Horn (Holger Lowenadler), using his newfound power to perform favors in a crude effort to impress the beleaguered man's beautiful daughter, symbolically named France (Aurore Clément). After
she is humiliated by his associates at a party to which Lucien had
escorted her, France accepts his comforting caresses, and the two
become lovers. Ultimately, the exhausted and impotent Horn rouses
himself enough to confront his tormentors at their headquarters,
whereupon he disappears from the film entirely. Lucien is dispatched
to evict the rest of the family, France and her aged grandmother
(Thérèse Gieshe), but when the German soldier leading the patrol
insults him for pocketing a watch he had previously given Horn,
Lucien suddenly shoots him and helps the refugees escape to the
countryside. The film concludes with a series of carefully composed,
idyllic scenes depicting the trio establishing a domestic routine while
hiding out in an abandoned farmhouse. Over a freeze frame of Lucien
contentedly chewing a piece of hay, a title informs us that "Lucien
Lacombe was arrested on October 12, 1944. Tried by a military court
of the Resistance, he was sentenced to death and executed."

The film's style and theme seem to reflect the post-1968
prodigality of the Nouvelle Vague. Malle himself was very much a

part of the initial energy that characterized New Wave filmmaking, having directed *Les amants* (1958) and *Zazie dans le métro* (1960), but only the opening credits of *Lacombe, Lucien*, a montage accompanied by jazz music of the boy bicycling home from work through the French countryside, recalls the lyrical evocation of freedom Truffaut created in *Jules and Jim*. Malle has acknowledged that this film is most deeply indebted to Marcel Ophuls's lengthy documentary about French collaboration during the Occupation, *The Sorrow and the Pity* (1971), as well as his own childhood memory of four Jewish boys who were betrayed by the priest who had been hiding them in a convent (the inspiration for *Au revoir les enfants* [1987]). In addition to expressing the disillusionment of many of the *Cahiers*/New Wave group at the time, the deliberately slow pace of *Lacombe, Lucien* functions in several significant ways: (1) it recapitulates the sense of boredom the characters frequently feel; (2) it suggests the apparent lack of will and direction in Lucien's shapeless existence; (3) it reinforces the historical process of the war winding down and the end of the Vichy government, just as the film begins to wind down after a few lively scenes early on (most notably, a hand-held panning shot of Lucien chasing after a chicken); (4) it encourages contemplation of the expressions of the main characters—Lucien's impassiveness, Horn's weariness, France's exquisiteness, the Gestapo crowd's evil banality—and meditation on the film's moral implications.

Malle's construction of Lucien's character carefully avoids easy interpretation. The seeds of the farm boy's brief career as a Nazi can be glimpsed in two "natural" moments depicting his daily village life, first when he skillfully uses his slingshot to kill a robin during a break from work and soon after when he captures the chicken that had eluded him and casually breaks its neck before turning it over to his mother. In a complementary manner, the tenderness he shows France the morning after their intimacy, gently caressing her naked back, deliberately recalls the earlier moment on the farm when he had patted the neck of a dead horse (fig. 24).[39] The moral ambiguity of Lucien's character is perfectly stated by Horn, who tells him, "It's odd. Somehow I can't bring myself to really hate you." To this point, perhaps two-thirds through the narrative, Lucien has been represented as a morally equivocal character in the conventional sense in which Coppola's Vito Corleone or Spielberg's Oskar Schindler are ambiguous characters. For the remainder of the film, however, he will become more like the other "lost objects" this book has described.[40]

FIGURE 24. *Lacombe, Lucien.* Courtesy Museum of Modern Art

Like the threesome in *Jules and Jim*, Lucien is sacrificed to the forces of history, his "out-of-itness" his primary crime. Malle signals his doom in a scene immediately following Horn's pronouncement about his character in which his mother delivers a miniature black coffin the Resistance has left as a warning to traitors. Lucien shrugs at the talisman and ignores her pleas to escape while there is still time. When he does ultimately flee, it is as if by accident, his sudden murder of the Gestapo officer necessitating his taking sides with France (and her grandmother). What had been Truffaut's nostalgia for lost idealism becomes here Malle's nostalgia for the careless freedom of lost youth, both destroyed by warfare and intolerance. The denouement of *Lacombe, Lucien* takes place in a timeless, edenic netherworld:

> *From this point on, there will be no further chronological progression, but a number of long sequences, as though one were patiently following the movements and gestures of the three people. They will never speak, or only rarely. Nor will there be any further reference to the war: in this sun-drenched setting, with no other human being present, we will have the feeling of being outside of time, outside of history, in a kind of eternity in which the most basic activities of life are repeated endlessly and monotonously over and over again.* (Malle and Modiano 116)

In a succession of ten scenes whose formal compositions are in sharp contrast with the hand-held camera and jittery framing found throughout the rest of the film, Malle imposes an artificial tranquility to memorialize these displaced lives. Perhaps the most striking of these brief episodes depicts Lucien perched in a tree on a beautiful sunny day, observing with apparent indifference as France searches for him, repeatedly calling out his name, never finding him.

The haunting mystery of this image of Lucien's simultaneous presence and absence is consecrated by the film's concluding freeze frame of his unfathomable face, accompanied by the languid melody of an unseen recorder and the notice of his death sentence. The casting of Pierre Blaise in the title role adds a further resonance. A country boy who had never acted before (according to some sources, he had never even seen a movie), he appears on screen unknown from previous performances—and, as fate would have it, virtually unseen forever more (fig. 25). After a brief celebrity following the film's release, he was killed in a high-speed automobile accident shortly after making one other picture, Dennis Berry's *The Great Frenzy* (1975). The casting of Thérèse Gieshe as the grandmother adds a further irony, perhaps recognized only by European audiences at the time. She had been a well-known stage actress in Nazi Germany and much admired by Hitler, who proclaimed her to be the perfect example of a great German actress. When informed of the Fuhrer's compliment, she immediately sent him a letter proclaiming her Jewish ancestry and left the country.

Casting also contributes to the memorious aura of *Daddy Nostalgia*. In this case, the enervated performance of Dirk Bogarde, returning to the screen after an absence of more than a decade, along with a minimal plot and subdued visual technique, combine to create the film's pervasive evocation of an irrecoverable past. Last seen as the very figure of decadence and exhaustion in such significant texts of the international art cinema as *The Damned* (1969), *Death in Venice* (1970), *The Night Porter* (1974), and *Despair* (1978), Bogarde again portrays a doomed man but one who remains charming despite his selfishness and who savors to the end the memories of his joyful life. His character thus perfectly represents Marc Vernet's description of "the experience of nostalgia," wherein "I contemplate with delectation the person that I was, that I believed I was, that I could have been, that I am no more, that maybe I never was, and yet with whom l love to identify" (58). As if redeemed by his unexpected reappearance in a major film, Bogarde invests his portrayal with none of the demonism, perversion, and jaded irony of his past roles; in Tavernier's paean to bourgeois life with all its indulgences, carelessness, and moral blindness, he is reborn as simply *human*.

Daddy Nostalgia manages to avoid sentimentality by adhering to "a principle of subtraction" (Paletz 48) evident in both the actors' performances—consisting of restrained movements, quiet intonations even when pained, angry, or sorrowful—and the narrative development, a simple story occasionally disrupted by brief flashbacks. Caroline (Jane Birkin), a divorced screenwriter, leaves behind her young boy (but not her work) in Paris when she is summoned to the hospital bedside of her father, who is recovering from a heart operation. She stays at her parents' Côte d'Azur villa to keep "Daddy" company during his recuperation. The film records the family's daily interactions, gradually revealing the daughter's lingering resentment of her father's neglect at the same time she conspires with him to undermine the restrictions imposed by her fear-

FIGURE 25. *Lacombe, Lucien*. Courtesy Jerry Ohlinger's

ful, deeply religious mother, Miche (Odette Laure). Caro eventually learns that Daddy has not long to live and, in the film's penultimate sequence—one that cannot be described as "climactic" because nothing particularly significant, no epiphany, occurs—takes him on a sentimental journey to Cannes that concludes with a gentle, intimate conversation at a gas station. Soon after she returns to Paris, she receives a call informing her that Daddy has died.

The film's theme might be equally applied to *Jules and Jim* and *Lacombe, Lucien.* "The sweetness of life," Daddy tells Caro at the end of their day together, "is very perishable." Whether this is a particularly French attitude goes beyond the scope of my expertise, though I suspect that in the cinema it has its roots in the poetic realism of Vigo, Renoir, Prévert, and Carné in the 1930s. Here, the ideas of renunciation and diminishing options are explicitly conveyed through the denouement. As Caro proposes a farewell "CocaCola for three," her taxi arrives early, leaving no time for tender words or embraces. After she exits from the right of the frame and Miche the left, the scene concludes with a long shot of Daddy, his back to the camera, looking out towards the sea—the film's very last image of him (fig. 26). When Caro returns to Paris, his is the last message on her answering machine, an already distant voice marking the presence of his absence, expressing his love for her and wishing her good night. Another male voice—Tavernier's, which had also begun the film by describing Caro's dream about pushing her father in a wheelbarrow on a fantastical world tour— takes over the narration, telling how Daddy had spoken of happiness in the past tense as something that "had slowly crumbled and which he'd lost along the wayside. No doubt he'd have liked her to help pick up the pieces and reconstruct it."

Some critics, arguing from either a formalist or feminist perspective, have resisted this intrusive narration without recognizing how the film's ending inscribes Daddy as the phantom of the cinema and Caroline as the avatar of his memory. As his character reflects upon an individual history that has, like that of Truffaut's trio and Malle's young couple, temporarily transcended world war ("We danced all through the raids," he reminds Miche), the actor reflects a cinematic history that spans from Renoir (about whose father Caro is writing a mini-series) to Resnais (who directed Bogarde in *Providence* [1977]). Like Monroe Stahr and Lucien Lacombe, Daddy never dies on screen, in his last appearance never leaves the frame. The voiceover narration might as well be *his* voice, since it describes hopes and anxieties he had chosen to repress. In fact,

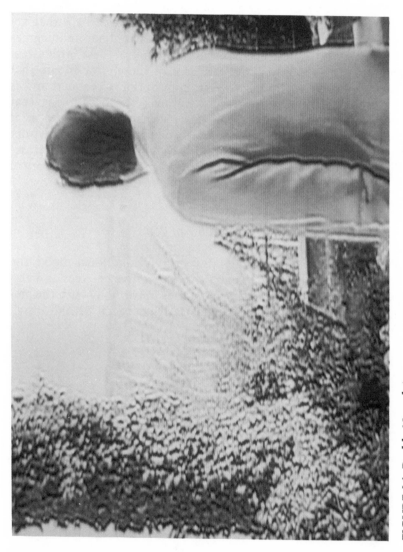

FIGURE 26. *Daddy Nostalgia*

however, the film's concluding voice is not his but Caro's—or rather, Jane Birkin's—singing the theme song (also the movie's alternate title), "These Foolish Things." Throughout the film's unspecified diegetic time Caroline has been working on a screenplay, presumably the biography of Auguste Renoir that she learns has been accepted when she returns to Paris. Or perhaps that yet unfinished script is to be the one that Daddy told her he imagines her writing, the filmed record of the experience of these bittersweet autumn days—something very much like the elegiac movie that Tavernier (who had lost his own father just prior to production) has now brought to an end. The concluding lyric to the song that accompanies the credits—a polished recording that echoes as it refines the spontaneous duet father and daughter had playfully shared on one of their outings—fulfills Daddy's wish to reconstruct "the sweetness of life" at the same time it preserves the memory of his character as another phantom of the cinema:

> Oh, how the ghost of you clings!
> These foolish things remind me of you.

Rather than a cheap sentimentality or a dysfunctional mood, the nostalgia articulated throughout Tavernier's film emerges as a creative source, one that brings the old tunes in harmony with the present and the traditions of classical narrative in touch with the modern artist's sense of loss.

CHAPTER EIGHT

◈

Conclusion: The Mystery and Melancholy of a Self

The posture that inaugurates knowledge is defined by a backward turn.

—Christian Metz

I take my title for this final chapter from de Chirico's well-known painting, *The Mystery and Melancholy of a Street* (1914), with its strange combination of nostalgia for Renaissance illusionism and dreamlike, hallucinatory images that refute the *quattrocento's* rational ordering of experience. Here the silhouetted girl with the hoop in the deserted piazza appears threatened by the disembodied figure outside the field of vision that interposes its gigantic shadow between her and the vanishing point. Neither the infinitely receding colonnade nor the empty furniture van provides refuge from the fate that seemingly awaits her. For me, the painting crystallizes the elements I have been associating with the phantom of the cinema: the specter of an unseen character whose shadow has a life of its own and whose identity remains "the key to it all," the vulnerable girl—herself a shadow—who unconsciously pursues him, the disquieting feeling summoned forth by the formal arrangement of the scene—the

139

sense of something missing, yet also something immanent, of still-
ness, yet also imminence.

The cinematic portraits that conclude my study share this same
aura of mystery and melancholy. They exhibit a persistent, unresolved ambiguity that haunts the spectator's imagination in the same
way that de Chirico's manipulation of conventional perspective and
defamiliarization of ordinary objects disturb the viewer's certainty
about the scene. Their motives and beliefs can neither be encom-
passed by the typologies associated with allegory or Hollywood cinema nor dismissed as the arbitrary, frivolous, or irrelevant ascrip-
tions of human identity associated with postmodernist narrative.
Frequently, as with the protagonists of such otherwise different films
as Istvan Szabo's *Mephisto* (1981), Steven Soderbergh's *sex, lies, and
videotape* (1989), and Jaco Van Dormael's *Toto the Hero* (1992), the
phantom of the cinema, above all, remains a mystery to himself. Van
Dormael's narrator believes his identity—and therefore his birthright
and his life—has been stolen from him in the cradle; his sometimes
comic, sometimes tortured quest to recover it finally culminates in
his triumphant assassination as he deliberately impersonates his
absent nemesis. "Am I supposed to recount all the points in my life
leading up to this moment and then hope that it's coherent, that it
makes some sense to you?" Graham asks Ann in Soderbergh's film.
"It doesn't make sense to me!" The melancholy that afflicts such
characters stems partly from this lack of self-understanding but also
from a fatality and isolation that mark their ontology as insubstantial,
shimmering images on the screen. "What do they want from me?"
the talented but vain Nazi collaborator Hendrik Höfgen (Klaus Maria
Brandauer) asks while trying to elude the blinding white spotlight of
the final close-up in *Mephisto* (fig. 27). "After all, I'm only an actor."
Another performer, frozen in time and speaking out of character in
Woody Allen's *The Purple Rose of Cairo* (1985), makes a similar
point. "Go with the real guy," the jaded Countess advises Cecilia
from her black-and-white movie-within-the-movie. "We're limited."
The characters I have been describing throughout this book are not
only doomed by historical, psychological, political, or biological forces
within the diegesis; they also appear "limited" by the very material
terms of their existence—their own two-dimensionality and the inex-
orable process of their unwinding through the projector. In such circumstances, the comedy of Allen's *Purple Rose*, no less than that of
its silent ancestor, Keaton's *Sherlock, Jr.* (1924), and French cousin,
Toto the Hero, or the nostalgia previously traced in Truffaut, Malle,
and Tavernier, inevitably turns bittersweet.

FIGURE 27. *Mephisto*

If there is a common bond among the characters identified here as "phantoms of the cinema," it may be expressed in the intensification of their metacinematic dilemma: while posing as the living, they exist only through their flickering traces on the screen. Even when the film represents a real person, as in *The Thin Blue Line*, these protagonists seem at pains to transcend the transparency of their own *recorded performances*, which is to say, their inherent *fictionality*. Always disembodied and displaced by the process of filmic signification, often dissociated, disturbed, or disillusioned within the diegesis—they remain in some sense "out of it," unable to escape from their roles into *being*. They become profoundly "convincing," to recall the actor Spegel's phrase in *The Magician*, only when they are revealed, as in Szabo's terrifying freeze frame of Hofgen's brightly illuminated face, as the ghosts of their own presented selves. In the brief examples that remain, we may continue to observe how some other rhetorical strategies specific to the cinema are used to render the mystery and melancholy of the characters' predicament.

VOICEOVER NARRATION IN MALICK'S
BADLANDS AND *DAYS OF HEAVEN*

In a very curious way, Terrence Malick has himself become a kind of phantom of the cinema. The director and screenwriter for what can arguably be described as the most original and accomplished first two films by an American director since Welles made *Citizen Kane* and *The Magnificent Ambersons* (1942), he has all but disappeared from the scene since *Days of Heaven* (1978). He has taken up apparently permanent residence in Paris, leaving behind only his cameo role in *Badlands* (1973) as a man holding blueprints who is turned away from the rich man's house (another instance of proleptic irony) and occasional rumors of works-in-progress.[41] His films evoke a corresponding sense of remoteness, most prominently through the use of long lens cinematography and voiceover narration that often seems dissociated from the diegetic images. Especially in *Badlands*, the lack of depth afforded by the telephoto shots contributes to a perception of the literal flatness of the characters, who appear strangely isolated from their natural surroundings, as when Kit (Martin Sheen) introduces himself to Holly (Sissy Spacek) in the opening scene, striking a series of poses against the blurred background of leafy trees immediately behind him. From this distorted perspective, the runaway couple cannot make significant progress even when speeding towards the camera in their stolen Cadillac across the vast plains. Lacking charm ("personality," Holly calls it in her narration, noting without regret her own deficiency), sensitivity ("I didn't feel shame or fear, just kinda blah," she reports shortly after Kit kills the friend who had sheltered them), or insight ("I made up my mind never to tag along with the hell-bent type," she concludes near the end), Holly must rely on second-hand phrases borrowed from schoolbooks like *Kon Tiki* or romance magazines. Like the language they adopt, the protagonists' behavior consists of empty gestures (Kit politely opens doors for people, Holly responds to Kit's murdering her father by slapping him), unconvincing role-playing, and phatic communication, devoid of content (Henderson 40). Thus, at various moments Kit refers to Holly as "Red," "Priscilla," "Tex," and "Mildred" without drawing any reply (although she does object to his calling her "stupid" after they have sex early in the film). Although less passive, Kit seems equally banal, lacking in any biographical detail except for a passing comment, barely audible, implying that he has served in Korea. His own self-image derives from his supposed resemblance to James Dean, a double whom he imitates poorly when he behaves respectfully with elders and offers wise advice to his imagined admirers: "Listen to your parents and teachers. They got a line on most things. . . . Try to keep an open mind. . . .Consider the minority opinion, but try to get along with the majority of opinion once it's accepted." In his increasingly desperate need to confirm his own existence—impossible in any film, but particularly so in one that foregrounds its own artifice and that withholds the identity of its true-life source, the mass murderer Charles Starkweather—Kit compulsively attempts to memorialize events in his life: saving a rock as a souvenir of the couple's first love-making, launching a balloon containing a packet of what Holly calls "some of our little tokens and things," burying another bucket of trinkets that "somebody might dig up in a thousand years and wouldn't they wonder," building a rock cairn to mark the spot where he is finally apprehended, handing out personal effects—a comb, a pen—to his captors, and, most significant in their reflexive aspect, twice preserving his voice in the form of homemade *recordings*, both of which insist that he and Holly have had "fun." Sensing the doom that awaits him, he seeks to become, like Bergman's Spegel, "convincing" as a ghost.

Compared to their cinematic progenitors, Arthur Penn's Bonnie Parker and Clyde Barrow, Holly and Kit seem pathetic, listless shadows. The film's formal construction of certain moments may lend grandeur, dignity, or mythic dimension to their experience—as in the fire sequence that concludes the first part of the narrative, the telephoto long shot of Kit with his rifle slung over his shoulders gazing at the horizon (an allusion to Dean's last role in Stevens's *Giant* [1956]), and the night scene of the pair illuminated by the car's headlights as they dance to Nat King Cole's "A Blossom Fell"—but the characters themselves are never redeemed, unlike the heroes of *Bonnie and Clyde* (1967), by their brief celebrity, their communal and class loyalties, or their undying love for each other. Malick seems to employ a majestic, epic style (in *Days of Heaven* as well) precisely to illustrate the tawdriness and emptiness of his protagonists' lives. The film's melancholy emanates from Kit and Holly's pervasive shallowness; its mystery lies in the very vacancy conveyed by their thoughts and deeds amidst the vast landscape (fig. 28).

Holly's voiceover narration expresses a totally insufficient response to the events she describes, as if Nancy Drew were narrating *Hiroshima, Mon Amour* (1959). Her first words situate her in a time and place far removed from her harrowing experience as a fifteen-year-old: "Little did I realize that what began in the alleys and backways of this quiet town would end in the Badlands of Montana." This laconic voice speaking after the fact persists till the very end, when her own fate is revealed: "Myself, I got off with probation and a lot of nasty looks. Later, I married the son of the lawyer who defended me." At several points, she notes her own sense of detachment: "The world was like a faraway planet to which I could never return"; "In the distance, I saw a train making its way silently across the plain, like the caravan in *The Adventures of Marco Polo*." Conventionally, such distanciation provides for both rhetorical grace and narrative insight, but Holly speaks almost exclusively in clichés and platitudes ("Better to spend a week with one who loved me for what I was than years of loneliness"; "We lived in utter loneliness, neither here nor there"). Her discourse never adequately explains the circumstances or expresses useful insights ("Suddenly I was thrown into a state of shock. Kit was the most trigger-happy person I'd ever met. . . . It all goes to show how you can know a person and not really know him at the same time"), never cues the spectator's emotions ("He dreaded the idea of being shot dead alone, he said, without a girl to scream out his name"). While the intense effect of Emmanuele Riva's narration in *Hiroshima, Mon Amour* follows from her voice's capacity to conjure up historical images and past desires, Holly's dreamy monotone becomes haunting rather than

FIGURE 28. *Badlands*

boring precisely because she herself seems so unhaunted by memory.

The film's most reflexive scene—a montage of antique photographs depicting various unrelated images[42]—compounds the defining element of presence/absence in Holly's narration. Kit has just said hello on his way to some task during their idyllic interlude in the forest, but she has ignored him, lost in thought:

> One day, while taking a look at some vistas in dad's stereopticon, it hit me that I was just this little girl, born in Texas, whose father was a sign painter, who had just only so many years to live. It sent a chill down my spine, and I thought: where would I be this very moment if Kit had never met me? or killed anybody? This very moment. If my mom had never met my dad? if she'd never died? And what's the man I'll marry gonna look like? What's he doing this very minute? Is he thinking about me now, by some coincidence, even though he doesn't know me? Does it show on his face? For days afterward, I lived in dread. Sometimes I wished I could fall asleep and be taken off to some magical land where this never happened.

In this reverie provoked by her solitary gazing at the still images, Holly does momentarily enter a "magical land," but one that reveals only questions, not answers. The ghosts of her parents and the specter of Kit's nearby presence give way to the fantastic vision of her future husband and domestic bliss, signified by Malick's zoom in on the picture of a young cavalry soldier kissing a girl during the last part of her monologue. Inviolate and opaque, Holly recedes from the spectator's view, beyond comprehension but still present in the sound of her voice trying to construct a future self.

While it is clear that Holly is an unreliable narrator, it may remain uncertain whether *Badlands* is an ambiguous text, one that "raises a question in the reader's/viewer's mind which it fails to answer, and where the raising and the nonanswering seem to have been intentional" (Currie 274). In this case, the question centers on character, the source and meaning of Kit's pathology and Holly's acquiescence. Despite the suggestiveness of the film's title and startling natural imagery or the characters' momentary flashes of sensitivity (such as Holly's observation that "when the leaves rustled overhead it was like the spirits were whispering about all the little things that bothered them" and Kit's response to Nat King Cole's performance: "Boy, if I could sing a song like that, if I could sing a song about the way I feel right now, it'd be a hit"), *Badlands* resists any psychological or ideological explanation for the protagonists' behavior. Malick's representation of character thus coincides with Welles's in *Citizen Kane*—without even the "dollar book Freud." Were we to find a "Rosebud," Malick seems to ask, would it really matter? The film's final exchange provides the answer. On the flight back to face trial, Kit ingratiates himself by admiring the sheriff's hat. "You're quite an individual, Kit," the lawman says. Smiling at the compliment, Kit replies, "Think they'll take that into consideration?"

The voiceover narration in *Days of Heaven* superficially resembles that of *Badlands*. Again the speaker (Linda Manz, in her first film role) is young, female, and basically a passive observer of violent events, but the girl who narrates *Days of Heaven* (her name is given in the credits as "Linda," but like all the other characters in the diegesis—her brother Bill, his lover Abby, the Farmer, and the Foreman—she is represented as a type, "the Girl") responds more sensitively than Holly to her surroundings, expresses her feelings more authentically, and displays more compassion for others. Although she remains a minor character in the film's plot and actually witnesses considerably less of the action than Holly, her discourse seems more reliable, more in tune with that of the implied author, Malick. Whereas Holly has been described as a haunting figure primarily because she is so unhaunted by the past, Linda recalls everything, sees spooks everywhere. Her narration begins with the memory of her former life in Chicago:

> It us'ta just be me and my brother. We us'ta do things. We had fun. We us'ta roam the streets. There was people suffering, pain and hunger. Some people their tongues were hanging outa their mouth. He us'ta juggle apples. He us'ta amuse us.

Over a montage sequence depicting a train filled with workers travelling across the countryside, accompanied by non-diegetic steel guitar music, the girl describes an acquaintance never seen in the film:

> I met this guy named Ding Dong. He told me the whole earth is going up in flames. Flames'll come out of here and there. They'll just rise up. . . . There's gonna be creatures runnin' every which way, some of them burnt, half their wings burned. People are gonna be screamin' and hollerin' for help. See, the people who have been good, they're gonna go to heaven and escape all that fire. . . . But if you've been bad, God don't even hear you. He don't hear you talkin'.

In this vision of apocalypse that seems so incongruous with the grandeur of the train silhouetted against the blue sky as it crosses a high trestle and shots that follow of the migrants arriving at a spacious wheat farm, Linda's imaginative version of a familiar tale heard second-hand becomes a chilling ghost story, one that anticipates rather than imitates the tragic events—murder, plague, and fire—about to unfold. Profoundly influenced by what might be called "the metaphysics of Ding Dong," a doomsday theology that also informs her opening monologue, her subsequent narration is replete with original speculations ("I've been thinking what to do with my future. I could be a mud doctor, checking out the earth, underneath"), mystical perceptions ("The sun looks ghostly when there's a mist on the river and everything's quiet. I never knowed it before"), and melancholy thoughts ("I think the devil was on the farm").

Linda Manz's distinctive New York accent, rather than a distracting anomaly as some reviewers found it, serves to underscore her radical displacement from the diegesis. In contrast to Sissy Spacek's Texas drawl, which fits perfectly the western milieu of *Badlands*, Linda's nasal tone and pronounced inflections reinforce her marginal relation to the action and vulnerability to forces beyond her control. At the same time, her child's voice persistently seeks to comprehend the situation and exhibits compassion for all the other characters (fig. 29). Consider her reflections on the Farmer (Sam Shepard, also in his first major film role):

> This farmer, he had a big spread and a lotta money. Whoever was sittin' in the chair when he come around, why'd they stand up and give it to him? Warn't no harm in him. You'd give him a flower, he'd keep it forever. He was headed for the boneyard any minute, but he wasn't squawkin' about it. Like some people. In one way I felt sorry for him. 'Cause he had nobody to stand out for him, be by his side, hold his hand when he needs attention or something. That's touchin'.

Holly never expresses any sympathy for the victims in *Badlands*; her descriptions of the forest and prairies remain equally detached, repeating the pat phrases of *Reader's Digest* and *National Geographic*. "There wasn't a plant in the forest that didn't come in handy"; "Through desert and mesa across endless miles of open range, we made our headlong way." While these expository passages refer less to the natural environment than to other (literary) texts,

FIGURE 29. *Days of Heaven.* Courtesy Museum of Modern Art

Linda describes the world "fresh," infused with her own active imagination and occupied by mysterious spirits. Holly's is the voice of Tom Sawyer—grammatical, respectable, conventional; Linda's is the voice of Huckleberry Finn.[43]

> Some sights that I saw was really spooky that it gave me goose pimples. I felt like cold hands touchin' the back of my neck and, well, it coulda been they was comin' after me or somethin'. I remember this guy, his name was Black Jack. He died. He only had one leg and he had died. And I think that was Black Jack makin' those noises.

Like Huck, she narrates these words from the precarious freedom afforded by a raft that takes the outlaw trio downriver. As Malick's camera drifts by a group of shadowy men on shore warming themselves by a midnight fire, the spectator listens to the disembodied voice of a little girl exiled from "days of heaven" on the farm and shares her search for the ghost of Black Jack (the phantom descendant of Ding Dong) hovering on the horizon.

Like *Badlands, Days of Heaven* incorporates a self-reflexive diegetic scene in which the narrator becomes a spectator beguiled by the film apparatus. Whereas Holly speculated on her own personal fate as she stared through the stereopticon, Linda again expounds on the devil's role in human fate ("he just sits there and laughs and watches while you're there all tied up and snakes are eatin' your eyes out") while watching the newly arriving passengers restrained by ropes in Chaplin's *The Immigrant* (1917). Enchanted by an image that reflects the tangled fate of the three adults who surround her somewhere in the darkness, her rapt gaze reproduces precisely the effect André Bazin used to describe Chaplin: "unlimited imagination in the face of danger" (148).[44] As her commentary concludes, Malick cuts to a brief shot of the girl's enraptured face illuminated by the flickering light of the projector immediately behind her. Having conjured up the ghosts of Ding Dong and Black Jack, she becomes herself, in this moment, a phantom of the cinema.

The film's closing long shot depicts Linda's small figure receding into the distance while her commentary reflects once more on the fate of another "character," an unnamed friend whom she had met on the farm and with whom she now sets off along the railroad tracks in search of further adventures:

FIGURE 30. *Days of Heaven*

This girl, she didn't know where she was going or what she was goin' to do. She didn't have no money or anything. Maybe she'd meet up with a character. I was hopin' things would work out for her. She was a good friend of mine.

Days of Heaven thus concludes with this mythic evocation of the open road, the vagabond, like Chaplin's Tramp, undaunted by experience, ever hopeful in the ghostly blue light of an American dawn. The image fades to black before the girls disappear from view (fig. 30).

DRAMATIC MONOLOGUE IN *FIVE EASY PIECES*

Bob Rafelson's *Five Easy Pieces* (1970) also concludes with a long shot of the open road, a highway in the Pacific Northwest down which the enigmatic protagonist disappears into an uncertain future. Rafelson signifies the mystery and melancholy of his antihero, Bobby Dupea (Jack Nicholson), by maintaining an unusually long take from a fixed camera as the semi that Bobby has hitched a ride with slowly drives off towards the vanishing point. More clearly than many of the texts studied here, *Five Easy Pieces* follows a character-centered script (co-written by Rafelson and Adrien Joyce), almost a case study of the apparently self-destructive behavior of a classically trained pianist who all but abandons his musically talented family for an itinerate working class lifestyle. Alternately charismatic and crude, Bobby exhibits a deep frustration that sometimes expresses itself through rage, as in his withering tirade at a waitress who fails to comply with his order for a chicken salad sandwich, and at other times through sullen silence, as when, in the final scene, he bolts from his pregnant girlfriend Rayette (Karen Black) without saying a word. Earlier, Rayette had called him "about the moodiest man I've ever been with"; her last words to him as she enters the appropriately named Gulf station are, "Sure you don't want anything?" Whatever it is he restlessly yearns for the audience never learns. Like Charles Foster Kane, Bobby inherits enormous cultural advantages but disdains their value; he is also a man who wants to be loved by others but seems incapable of returning love. A true product of his turbulent era, he clings to a fierce sense of integrity (one may recall Welles's character bellowing at the departing Geddes, "I'm Charles Foster Kane!") without truly knowing who he is. In the final analysis, neither does the spectator.

Five Easy Pieces does not often relate the ambiguity of its protagonist to the presence/absence of the cinematic signifier in any clearly self-conscious way. Bobby's status as an artist *manque*—he pounds out strident chords on a battered upright hijacked during a freeway traffic jam and later relishes the outraged reaction of his family's intellectual friends when he defends the music he once played in a Las Vegas strip joint—may suggest some broad association with the populist roots of movie-making. In two scenes, however, the film does seem to remind the spectator of its own particular signifying practice. The first occurs when Bobby plays a Chopin étude at the request of Catherine (Susan Anspach), a musician staying at the family's Puget Sound estate who is his brother's fiancée. The slow tracking shot over hands, instruments, flowers, artifacts, and family portraits amounts to a kind of cinematic still life. Anthony Macklin has pointed out how this set piece "calls attention to the very process of creating an aesthetic effect" (7). The spectator, like Catherine, may initially respond to the moment as a deeply moving revelation of Bobby's heretofore repressed artistic side, forgetting both the complementary effects of the camera and the fact—standard in fictional narratives about musicians—that Jack Nicholson is faking his performance, just as his character claims no real involvement once the piece is finished. "I faked a little Chopin," Bobby tells his solitary listener, "you faked a little response." The seduced and betrayed Catherine, in this instant the educated double of the easily manipulated Rayette (who derives similar pleasure from listening to Tammy Wynette recordings), also becomes a surrogate for the film audience that has been left without adequate means for interpreting a seemingly intimate experience now irrevocably lost.

This impromptu recital is followed by another ambiguous tour de force amounting to a verbal rather than musical monologue. After Catherine rejects him for being incapable of loving anything or anyone, especially himself, Bobby takes his paralyzed father to a secluded, beautiful spot near the water and tries to explain his rootless, empty existence. The sequence begins with an extreme long shot of the two figures silhouetted against a dreary late afternoon sky. Crouched in front of the wheelchair, shivering with the cold, Bobby struggles to explain himself:

> I don't know if you'd be particularly interested in hearing anything about me, my life. Most of it doesn't add up to much I could relate as a way of life you'd approve of. I move around a lot, not because I'm looking for anything, really, but 'cause I'm getting away from things that get bad if I stay. Auspicious beginnings, you know what I mean? . . . I'm trying to imagine

FIGURE 31. *Five Easy Pieces*

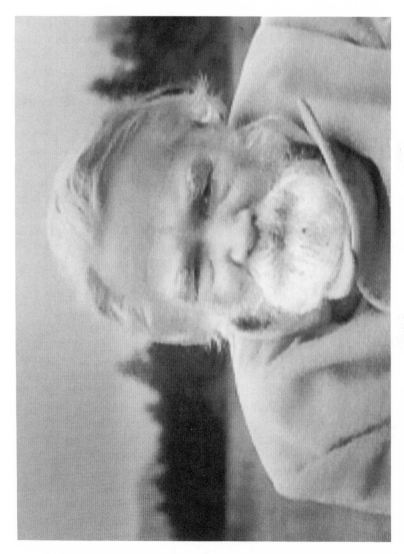

FIGURE 32. *Five Easy Pieces*

your half of this conversation. My feeling is, I don't know, that if you could talk we wouldn't be talking. That's pretty much the way that it got to be before I left. Are you all right? I don't know what to say. Tita suggested that we try to, I don't know. I think that she feels that we have got some understanding to reach. She totally denies the fact that we were never that comfortable with one another to begin with. The best I can do is apologize. We both know that I was never that good at it anyway. I'm sorry it didn't work out.

This monologue, consuming two and a half minutes of film time, resolves none of the enigmatic melancholy embedded in the representation of Bobby's character to this point.[45] Although he chokes with tears more than once, his speech brings neither reconciliation nor catharsis. Rafelson's editing confirms this judgment. After an establishing two-shot, father and son never again appear together in the frame. The camera cuts away three times from the slight high angle close-up of Bobby to brief close-ups of his father's unmovable, inscrutable bearded face (figs. 31, 32). Instead of providing formal closure by returning to the opening two-shot after Bobby's subdued apology, the scene abruptly shifts to a day or two later and his sister Tita calling out to him to say goodbye.

The verbal text itself is also inconclusive, leaving more questions still unanswered. Was Bobby really a mediocre musician, or is his final admission just a cop-out? And what does "auspicious beginnings" mean? The phrase actually makes little sense as an explanation for leaving before things get bad. But the most certain measure of Bobby's opaque character lies in Mr. Dupea's expressionless countenance. Seated, immobile, incapable of interceding either to comfort or upbraid his son, excluded from the frame for nearly the entire monologue, his mostly unseen presence refigures both the film spectator's position and the unfathomable meaning of the elusive character before him. By discarding conventional classical editing (shot/reverse shot) in favor of cameras at right angles, Rafelson's cutting places Mr. Dupea precisely halfway between the audience and the phantom object of their gaze. As Bobby's behavior continues to mystify, no other character offers privileged insight into his character. Perhaps his sister offers the most promising clue, albeit unwittingly, when she describes her piano as having "absolutely no objectionable idiosyncrasies." Human beings, the film suggests, are quite different, and Bobby remains idiosyncratic to the end.

THE "LOOK BACK" IN *THE LACEMAKER*

No film character comes to mind who more fully represents the mystery and melancholy I have been describing than the protagonist of Claude Goretta's *The Lacemaker* (*La dentellière*, 1977). The heroine is Béatrice (Isabelle Huppert), nicknamed "Pomme," a shy young shopgirl in a Paris beauty parlor. The narrative depicts her first romance: a well-bred Sorbonne student named François (Yves Beneyton) meets her while on vacation in Normandy and rejects her some months later, bringing on an emotional and physical collapse. As the seasons shift from spring to late autumn and the scenery from seacoast resort to the crowded Parisian streets, the film seemingly invites interpretation as a modern parable of lost innocence, a Marxist allegory on the plight of the working class, or even a clinical study of depression and mental breakdown. Goretta's concerns, however, prove less moralistic than those of Eric Rohmer, less political than Jean-Luc Godard's or Alain Tanner's, and less intellectual than Alain Resnais's. His deepest interest lies with Béatrice herself, with who she once was and who she has become, with what she has lost and, possibly, what she has gained.

In most respects, Béatrice appears the very opposite of Bobby Dupea, trusting where he is cynical, domestic where he is nomadic, contented where he is frustrated, caring where he is ruthless, innocent where he is guilty. For much of the film, in fact, she conforms to the typology of *un coeur simple*. Only in the film's closing sequence, particularly in the final tracking shot and close-up, is her complexity fully revealed. The narrative initially contrasts her with her co-worker Marylène (Florence Giorgetti), a slightly older and far more experienced beautician who, like her namesake Marilyn Monroe (whose poster adorns a wall in her apartment), is blonde, restless, seductive, and a compulsive *poseur*. In the second movement, after Marylène deserts her for a new man during their sojourn in Cabourg, Béatrice meets François—another opposite—whose tall, thin frame and dark t-shirt and jeans visually contrast with her round face, petite figure, and white dress at the moment their romance begins. Attracted by what she calls his "considerateness," Pomme soon agrees to sleep with him, her first time with a man, and devotedly transforms his Paris flat into a cozy love nest. François, though self-absorbed and finally no less shallow than Marylène, is always courteous and genuinely well-meaning. His life with Béatrice seems epitomized in a scene where she tries to eat an apple silently (her nickname means "apple"—the biblical association seems deliber-

FIGURE 33. *The Lacemaker*

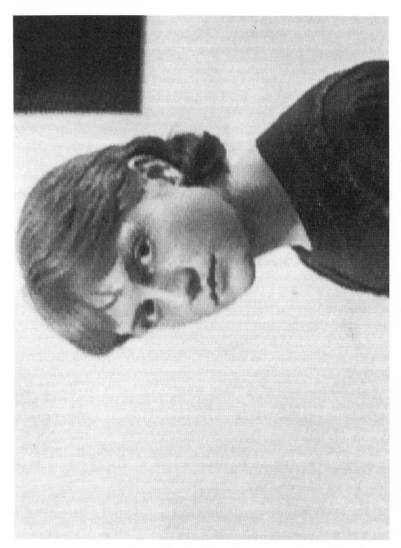

FIGURE 34. *The Lacemaker*

ate) without disturbing his studies, and he becomes bothered not so much by the sound as by her effort at self-effacement.

After depicting their tender courtship ("Take good care of her," Marylène tells François, "She's fragile") and apparently blissful relationship in Paris (François's leftist friends approve), Goretta details the subtle unraveling of their romance. In a high angle long shot foreshadowing their parting and mirroring the panoramic views of Cabourg when they first met, François rushes across a city boulevard, leaving Béatrice stranded on a pedestrian island. The film then crosscuts between François at home rehearsing a speech breaking off the affair and Béatrice walking back from work, the editing reinforcing their impending separation. Béatrice silently accepts the news, washing lettuce for the evening's meal while he explains how this will be best for both of them. In a rapid series of scenes at odds with the film's previous slow narrative pace, Béatrice returns to her mother's apartment (her father had abandoned the family when she was a child), becomes listless at work, physically ill and severely depressed (the critic Gillian Parker assumes that she is pregnant, but this point is never made explicit). One day, she collapses in the middle of a busy intersection.

The final sequence takes place four months later in a sanatorium where Béatrice has been convalescing. François reluctantly decides to pay a visit only after his two university friends agree to keep him company on the drive. When Béatrice walks down a long corridor towards the camera to greet him, her appearance is profoundly disturbing. She wears a shapeless black dress like a shroud; she moves and speaks mechanically, like the victim of a vampire's bite, drained of all her former charm. They pass the time together in a park filled with fallen yellow leaves, François filling the gap between them with small talk. When he asks what she has been doing since they parted, Béatrice tonelessly describes a trip to Greece with someone she met. François seems relieved to learn that she has taken new lovers, and they say goodbye with smiles. In the car before rejoining his friends, however, he weeps over the change that has come over her.

In the closing shot, the camera tracks behind Béatrice as she shuffles into the therapy room, sits alone at a corner table, and begins knitting in front of a bright poster of Mykonos (fig. 33). The truth behind the previous dialogue now becomes clear: her foreign travel was an illusion, a gesture of either contempt (mocking François's self-serving gullibility) or generosity (alleviating his remorse). The dolly moves closer and to the side of Béatrice until she slowly turns her head to gaze unblinkingly at the camera—and at *us*. Goretta holds this concluding close-up for what seems an unendurably long duration (actually about twenty-five seconds), allowing sufficient time to contemplate, as one would a painting, her enigmatic expression (fig. 34). In this paradigmatic instance of what Marc Vernet and Wheeler Dixon have defined as the "look back,"[46] the spectator confronts not simply the ambiguity of the wasted yet unyielding character at the final diegetic moment, but the ghost of her former self, Pomme, the plump and freckled girl who had once splashed carelessly in the sea. For a prolonged moment as well, the audience may experience the simultaneous alignment of the space of filming through Huppert's acknowledgment of the camera, the diegetic universe through Béatrice's solitary confinement, and the space of the theater through the spectators' impression that the character is looking directly at them (Vernet 49). Framed by the tight composition against a blank white wall with a small black square in the upper right, Béatrice's phantom image in the moment of projection also refigures "the returned gaze of the cinematic apparatus itself" (Dixon 2). You have to scrutinize that face, having been implicated by its testimony to a meaning beyond words. Is it the face of madness, of an isolated soul broken by society's injustice? Or is it the look of defiance and recrimination born of inarticulate rebellion? For me, Béatrice's "backward turn" expresses the shock of recognition (like Bartleby's "I know where I am" or Kurtz's "The horror, the horror") that follows knowledge of the world. Before any meaning becomes certain, however, the film's closing title intercedes, replacing the woman's haunting expression but reminding us that we have seen her before:

> He will have passed by her, right by her, without really noticing her, because she was one of those who gives no clues, one who has to be questioned patiently, one of those difficult to fathom.
> Long ago a painter would have made her the subject of a genre painting. She would have been a Seamstress
> > Water Girl
> > Lacemaker.

The text refers us to Vermeer's celebrated portraits, not only *The Lacemaker* (1669–70) alluded to in the tracking shot of Beatrice taking up her knitting as well as in the film's title, but also the less famous *The Girl with a Pearl Earring* (1665), whose pose Béatrice assumes in the final (nearly) still frame. In the latter painting, which focuses on the girl's character as she turns her head to gaze outward and not on the activity that absorbs her attention, Vermeer abandons the microscopic detail often seen in the works of his contemporaries (and evident in Goretta's opening tracking shot of a Parisian beauty parlor) for close scrutiny of the human face, the site, as Bergman has put it, of "the film's distinguishing mark and patent of nobility" (qtd. in Donner 242). The look back of the painting's subject rewards us with its eternal beauty and alertness; Béatrice's returned gaze, by contrast, rebukes us for not paying attention until it is too late.

My own "backward turn" over the pages I have written reveals the necessary indeterminacy and incompletion of my project. Adopting what Jameson has called postmodernism's "critique of the hermeneutic" (12) but still retaining a humanist's interest in the representational function of character, I have generally employed a hermeneutic approach to understanding how these texts themselves critique the efficacy of any definitive cinematic portrait other than one whose resistance to interpretation (as in the cases of Bobby and Béatrice) becomes the dominant element. If I have flinched at times from elaborating the psychological, cultural, political, and historical implications expressed by these characters, I have done so purposefully, cognizant of the perils. In their fleeting insubstantiality and unresolved ambiguity, the figures I have traced here both personify the signifying process that brings them to life and fulfill Tolstoy's intuition about the cinema's potential to bring narrative "closer to life." At the same time, they remind us that although the construction of character may ultimately be an illusion, it is a *necessary* illusion in order to sustain the desire to experience whatever might come next.

This study of film "phantoms" remains but a pinpoint within a spectrum of possible approaches to the analysis of character. My survey invites much further discussion of several topics I have touched upon, such as the impact of video reception and digitalized imaging, the rhetoric of character construction in particular genres, or historical developments in the representation of character. I have acknowledged at the outset that my taxonomy of character types is obviously incomplete, nor have I adequately considered the ideological aspects of character construction or thoroughly pursued theoretical comparisons with theater, literary fiction, and television. Instead, I have attempted to begin a discourse in a long-neglected field, hoping that others will test my assumptions and expand upon my examples.

In light of my own circumscribed horizons as well as the limitations of space, there is only one thing left to suggest, and that is how looking back at these films has rewarded my own close inspection with images of enduring beauty and portraits of haunting humanity beyond the assay of the most sophisticated academic theory. In the aura of this shimmering spectacle, I shall continue to gaze in awed silence.

NOTES

CHAPTER ONE.
THE PHANTOM OF THE CINEMA

1. In a recent article on spirit photography, which became a fashion under the influence of the late nineteenth-century Spiritualist movement, Tom Gunning describes how photography emerged as both material support for the new positivism and as "an uncanny phenomenon, one which seemed to undermine the unique identity of objects and people, endlessly reproducing the appearances of objects, creating a parallel world of phantasmatic doubles alongside the concrete world of the senses" (42–43). This attempt to document the presence of spirits marks the earliest and perhaps most eccentric example of the phantom aspect of the filmed image: its status as a "ghostly double" of the material world.

2. Each of these qualities becomes diminished in television transmission, which seeks to preserve the audience's faith in the presentness of the image. "The predominant myth of cinema, fostered by cinema itself, is that the images and sounds present reality. The equivalent myth of TV is that its broadcasts are immediate and live" (Ellis 77).

3. John Ellis has provided an excellent antidote to my simplified explanation here, one that underscores the play of presence/absence that is at the heart of my argument, by suggesting how the star system presents the paradox of people who are both ordinary and extraordinary: "The star is an impossible image, like the cinematic image. The star is tantalisingly close and similar, yet at the same time remote and dissimilar" (97–98).

4. The language of literature becomes antiquated less quickly than film images—in English, the process seems to take about a century—while Shakespeare's plays, though the language be dated, can be revived in modern dress or with whole scenes cut.

5. Wim Wenders employs a strikingly similar mirror shot when Travis (Harry Dean Stanton) addresses his long-lost wife (Nastassja Kinski) through a peep-show's one-way window in *Paris, Texas* (1984). As she approaches the window to search out his unseen presence, Travis's image is silhouetted over her shadowed face. In the rectangular frame-within-the-frame, Travis then shines the light of a small table lamp on his face so that Jane, now in darkness on the other side, can see him.

6. Although I do not contend that the director, Don Siegel, consciously employs the image for the reflexive function I have described, it does seem noteworthy that the mask alone remains on the screen during the closing credits as a reminder of the protagonist's notorious escape from view.

7. In what might be considered an additional permutation of presence/absence, this final shot evokes another profoundly disturbing moment of violence recorded on film, Abraham Zapruder's home movie of the Kennedy assassination. The viewer may recall, albeit subconsciously, that earlier terrifying vision of a world leader destroyed by a distant, anonymous sharpshooter. For a moment, despite our knowing de Gaulle's actual fate, the exploding "brain" of the melon makes his assassination seem possible.

CHAPTER TWO.
REFLEXIVITY AND CHARACTER IN *PERSONA*

8. See especially Susan Sontag's review article in *Sight and Sound*, 36.4 (autumn 1967),186–91, reprinted in her *Styles of Radical Will*; John Simon's chapter in *Ingmar Bergman Directs*, 208–310; and Paisley Livingston's *Ingmar Bergman and the Rituals of Art*, 180–220. A complete bibliography of critical responses to the film can be found in Birgitta Steene's *Ingmar Bergman: A Guide to References and Resources*,124–27. My own partial analysis of the film on which this chapter is based, "The Imaginary Signifier in Bergman's *Persona*," first appeared in *Film Criticism*, 2.2–3 (winter 1979).

9. Most studies of *Persona*, including my own, employ a movieola or video tape player to examine and, in some cases, to decipher the more ambiguous images, assuming that these details affect our comprehension on at least a subliminal level. This procedure may prove illuminating, especially during the rapidly edited sequences like the credits, but no definitive account of the film can afford to ignore the pace with which images are presented and withdrawn.

10. In Bergman's *The Passion of Anna* (1969) a similarly typed, personal letter falls into the hands of an unintended reader. This time, how-

ever, the close-up more conventionally maintains the mimetic illusion: the enlarged typescript displays variance among the keys and fragments of lines can be seen above and below the highlighted section.

11. Writing about the memorable picture of the Vietnamese monk reaching for the gasoline can, Sontag makes a point that applies equally to the photograph of the Warsaw ghetto child: "Photographing is essentially an act of non-intervention" (*Photography* 11). The newsreel of the bonze's self-immolation in *Persona* also contains the image of a photographer closing in to record the event.

CHAPTER THREE.
INCARNATIONS OF THE CONFIDENCE MAN

12. The text most often studied today is, in fact, itself a simulacrum of the original, not film but video cassette, its images reduced, cropped, and transmitted electronically, its narrative routinely interrupted by the viewer.

13. As I use the term here, "confidence" encompasses political, philosophical, and cultural as well as aesthetic associations. The mesmerizing power of the con man may illustrate the dangers of fascism (*A Face in the Crowd*), the desperate need for religious faith (*Elmer Gantry*), or the intoxication of media celebrity (*Talk Radio*, 1988), in addition to the mutual dependency existing between artist and audience. The most interesting films, of course, imply all of these dimensions.

14. This rhetorical question may illustrate a crucial distinction either between Bergman's sensibility and that of George Roy Hill or between the relative artistic freedom afforded by Svensk Filmindustri as opposed to the Hollywood system. In Hill's *Butch Cassidy and the Sundance Kid*, the fleeing outlaws become frustrated by the persistence of the lawmen pursuing them and repeatedly ask each other, "Who *are* those guys?" Viewed obscurely from great distance through a telephoto lens, the posse begins to assume the mythic proportions of the Greek furies until, in a moment that restores the movie to the quotidian, they draw close enough to be identified with certainty.

15. Quotations from the film have been taken from both the English subtitles and the published screenplay. I have chosen the phrasing that best suits my own prose but have in every case checked to make certain the meaning is the same in either form.

16. In the next chapter I will be discussing a modern remake of F. W. Murnau's silent vampire film, *Nosferatu*. Since the protagonist in this case is characterized as "undead," living a phantom existence, in effect Werner Herzog's copy represents what Bergman's Spegel might call "the shadow of

a shadow of a shadow." Fortunately, I will not elaborate this tortured logic any further.

17. Of the many books, articles, and reviews I have consulted, Paisley Livingston's *Ingmar Bergman and the Rituals of Art* most thoroughly elaborates the film's reflexivity by closely examining the denouement, although his attention to the final scene is largely confined to the swinging lantern in the closing long shot.

18. *House of Games* was filmed in Seattle, but none of my students or colleagues has been able to identify the city before the credits, nor do any of the reviews or articles I have seen make mention of the fact.

CHAPTER FOUR.
REVIVING THE UNDEAD

19. Coppola's version offers a superficial instance of reflexivity by having the Count first meet Mina in 1897 at a London exhibition of the newly invented cinematograph. His initial seduction proceeds in front of the primitive black-and-white images being projected for the curious crowd, but the reference seems purely historical rather than ontological and is not repeated.

20. Not loosely enough: Stoker's widow successfully prosecuted Murnau for copyright infringement, which may account for the disappearance of the original negative.

21. Herzog's portrait of the Count as witness to centuries of human sorrow anticipates Wim Wenders' representation of the angels who wander through Berlin in *Wings of Desire* (1988).

22. This scene recalls many similar hallucinatory moments in Herzog's work, most notably the response of the raftsman in *Aguirre, Wrath of God* upon first seeing a ship atop a tree and then being immediately shot by unseen natives: "That is no ship. That is no forest. This is no arrow."

CHAPTER FIVE.
THE SPY AND THE CIPHER

23. For a detailed analysis of the spy novel tradition and the influence of Conrad and Greene on le Carré's fiction, see David Monaghan, *The Novels of John le Carré*, 72–122.

24. Here is the passage from le Carré's novel: "What do you think spies are: priests, saints, and martyrs? They're a squalid procession of vain

fools, traitors too, yes; pansies, sadists and drunkards, people who play cowboys and Indians to brighten their rotten lives. Do you think they sit like monks in London balancing the rights and wrongs?" Ritt's film benefits from the pithier language, the broadening of the religious references, and, most of all, the compelling voice of Richard Burton.

25. It seems both odd and telling in regard to Reilly's moral and political ambiguity that the film aired as part of PBS's *Mystery* series rather than the seemingly more appropriate *Masterpiece Theatre* or *Great Performances*.

26. Allen's use of these real life "witnesses" undoubtedly involves parody of the technique as employed in Warren Beatty's *Reds* (1981).

27. Although my research was not exhaustive on this particular topic, I was surprised by the lack of consideration given to the film career of Bruno S., despite his unforgettable performances in *The Mystery of Kaspar Hauser* and Herzog's *Stroszek* (1977). None of the reference works on actors I consulted contained an entry on Bruno S., nor did the critical essays on *Kaspar Hauser* discuss in detail his particular contribution to the film's "mystery." I attribute this omission to the general lack of adequate terminology for analyzing film acting and the possible uncertainty about how to approach issues raised by Bruno's mental retardation or Herzog's alleged exploitation of him.

CHAPTER SIX.
DOCUMENTING CHARACTER IN
THE THIN BLUE LINE

28. Wheeler Winston Dixon cites Humphrey Bogart's digitalized appearance and top billing over John Lithgow and Isabella Rossellini in a 1995 HBO *Tales from the Crypt* episode as exemplifying how "an entire performance can now be created out of cannibalized imagery." He further speculates about "an entirely synthetic star being digitally constructed as a franchise possession by a studio or digital effects firm." See "The Digital Domain: Some Preliminary Notes on Image Mesh and Manipulation in Hyperreal Cinema/Video." *Film Criticism* 20.1–2 (fall/winter 1995–96), 55–66.

29. In *Representing Reality* (1991), Nichols revises these earlier categories of documentary, defining direct address as the expository mode and cinéma vérité as the observational mode.

30. The chief investigator in the Adams case, Gus Rose, had also led the interrogation of Oswald after the Kennedy assassination thirteen years earlier, although this fact is not mentioned in the film.

31. Asked by Bill Moyers to explain the "curious vacancy" created by the missing testimony of Adams's brother, Morris said that the man did testify, but because he was an alcoholic and unable to recall the particular events of a night four weeks earlier, he could not provide an ironclad alibi.

All Errol Morris quotations have been taken from this interview with Bill Moyers, April 26, 1989, for the *American Playhouse* television presentation of *The Thin Blue Line* on PBS.

32. Linda Williams's article refers to an unpublished paper by Charles Musser, "Film Truth: From 'Kino Pravda' to *Who Killed Vincent Chin?* and *The Thin Blue Line*," delivered at a conference at NYU in October, 1990, which argues that the prosecution saw Adams as a homosexual. No published review or article I have found directly raises this issue as it pertains to either the police investigation or Adams's possible reasons for remaining in Harris's company.

33. "There are many film makers who forget the human face is the starting point in our work. To be sure, we can become absorbed by the esthetic of the picture montage, we can blend objects and still lives into wonderful rhythms, we can fashion nature studies of astonishing beauty, but the proximity of the human face is without doubt the film's distinguishing mark and patent of nobility" (Ingmar Bergman qtd. in Donner 242).

34. According to John Pierson, the suit was settled without money changing hands "since the perceived success of the movie generated only imaginary dollars" (113).

CHAPTER SEVEN.
AVATARS OF MEMORY

35. Allen's published screenplay says, "*Not* everybody gets corrupted," which conveys a different sense than Hemingway's actual reading of the line. To my mind, the spoken version is more interesting for its apparent inconsistency, underscoring the ephemeral quality of Tracy's character in the film's penultimate moment.

36. A similar effect can be felt in watching Liza Minnelli's performance in *Cabaret* (1972), especially when Sally naively speaks of "divine decadence." Spectators may, in such moments, simultaneously recall the tragic trajectory of Judy Garland's career (at the time of the film's release) and Minnelli's own largely unfulfilled screen promise (now).

37. A similar instance of one character's absence signalling an act of violence on screen occurs when Elisabet steps on the shard of glass left by the departed Alma in *Persona*, briefly discussed in chapter two.

38. In his autobiography Kazan claims to have been conscious of the implications of this final shot: "It was the end, the fade-out of the film I was making and the end for me and my time as a director." His sense of the scene was either confirmed by or appropriated from an essay I had published in 1982 about *The Last Tycoon* and shared with him while he was working on the book. See *Elia Kazan: A Life*. New York: Knopf,1988, 721.

39. Malle and Patrick Modiano's published screenplay underscores this association by describing Lucien's gentle fondling of France as "the way one would pet an animal" (84).

40. Horn's character, too, is a kind of phantom, the ghost of his former self in Paris but also a surrogate father for Lucien, whose own father is absent from the film, a prisoner of war. Horn's abrupt disappearance from the film further underscores this aspect of his representation.

CHAPTER EIGHT.
CONCLUSION

41. Malick wrote a screenplay for the movie that eventually became *Great Balls of Fire* (1989) but was dismissed from the project before it went into production. *Sight and Sound* recently reported that he is currently making a screen version of James Jones's novel *The Thin Red Line* for Michael Medavoy's new company, Phoenix Pictures (March 1996, 4).

42. The images include a tree-lined canal, the Sphinx, a steamboat on a mountain lake, a mother and child, two women around a piano (color tinted), several people sitting on a lawn in front of a house, and a cavalry soldier kissing a girl. Only the last picture seems directly related to the content of Holly's simultaneous narration.

43. Malick has acknowledged his indebtedness to Twain as well as other children's books like *The Hardy Boys* and *Swiss Family Robinson*, "all involving an innocent in a drama over his or her head" (Walker 82).

44. I am indebted to Lynn A. Higgins for citing the Bazin quotation in reference to the insertion of the same scene from *The Immigrant* in Malle's *Au revoir les enfants* (1987). See her *New Novel, New Wave, New Politics*, 195.

45. Joel Siegel has pointed out (derisively) how this scene resembles "the James Dean–Raymond Massey number" (12) at the end of *East of Eden* (1955), but the differences are instructive. The father in Kazan's film is not totally unresponsive to his son's presence; in fact, his faint smile signifies a kind of benediction and brings closure to the film. In contrast, as I have shown, Bobby's confession is ambiguous and without effect. Cal (the Dean

character) is represented as a complex but nonetheless comprehensible young man in *East of Eden*, and his estrangement is resolved in this final scene. Bobby, however, remains a phantom figure doomed (like Harker in Herzog's *Nosferatu*) to journey far from home.

46. "Our primary model must be as follows: an actor (just one actor) faces the camera and, close to it, fixes a point situated where the camera is" (Vernet 49).

WORKS CITED
AND CONSULTED

◈

Andrew, Dudley. *Film in the Aura of Art*. Princeton: Princeton UP, 1984.

———. "The Neglected Tradition of Phenomenology in Film Theory." *Movies and Methods*, Vol II. Ed. Bill Nichols. Berkeley: U of California P, 1985, 626–32.

Andrews, Nigel. "Dracula in Delft." *American Film* 4.1 (1978): 32–38.

Badley, Linda. *Film, Horror, and the Body Fantastic*. Westport: Greenwood,1995.

Barbow, John D. *German Expressionist Film*. Boston: Twayne,1982.

Barr, Alan P. "The Unraveling of Character in Bergman's *Persona*." *Literature/Film Quarterly* 15.2 (1987): 123–36.

Barthes, Roland. *S/Z*. Trans. Richard Miler. New York: Hill and Wang,1974.

———. *Camera Lucida*. Trans. Richard Howard. New York: Hill and Wang,1981.

Baudry, Jean-Louis. "The Apparatus: Metapsychological Approaches to the Impression of Reality in the Cinema." *Film Theory and Criticism*. 4th ed. Ed. Gerald Mast, Marshall Cohen, and Leo Braudy. New York: Oxford UP,1992. 690–707.

Bayer, William. *The Great Movies*. New York: Grosset and Dunlap, 1973.

Bazin, André. *What Is Cinema?* 2 vols. Trans. Hugh Gray. Berkeley: U of California P, 1967.

Bellour, Raymond. "The Unattainable Text." *Screen* 16 (autumn 1975): 19–27.

Bergman, Ingmar. *Images*. New York: Arcade,1994.

———. *Persona and Shame*. New York: Grossman, 1972.

———. *Four Screenplays of Ingmar Bergman*. New York. Simon and Schuster,1960.

Billington, Michael. "A Spy Story Even James Bond Might Envy." *New York Times* 15 Jan. 1984, sec. 2: 27.

Bjorkman, Stig, Torsten Manns, and Jonas Sima. *Bergman on Bergman*. New York: Simon and Schuster, 1973.

Blair, John G. *The Confidence Man in Modern Fiction*. New York: Barnes & Noble, 1979.

Bordwell, David. *Film Art: An Introduction*. 3rd ed. New York: McGraw Hill, 1990.

———. *Making Meaning*. Cambridge: Harvard UP, 1989.

———. *Narration in the Fiction Film*. Madison: U of Wisconsin P, 1985.

Branigan, Edward. *Point of View in the Cinema*. New York: Mouton,1984.

Braudy, Leo. *The World in a Frame*. Garden City, NY: Anchor,1977.

Campbell, Paul Newell. "The Reflexive Function of Beraman's *Persona*." *Cinema Journal* 19.1 (winter 1979): 71–85.

Carroll, Noël. *Mystifying Movies*. New York: Columbia UP, 1978.

Cavell, Stanley. *The World Viewed*. Enlarged ed. Cambridge: Harvard UP, 1979.

Chatman, Seymour. *Coming to Terms: The Rhetoric of Narration in Fiction and Film*. Ithaca: Cornell UP, 1990.

———. *Story and Discourse: Narrative Structure in Fiction and Film*. Ithaca: Cornell UP, 1978.

Cixous, Hélène. "The Character of 'Character'." *New Literary History* 5.2 (winter 1974): 383–402.

Coates, Paul. *Film at the Intersection of High and Mass Culture*. New York: Cambridge UP, 1994.

Cohen, Hubert I. *Ingmar Bergman: The Art of Confession*. New York: Twayne, 1993.

Conrad, Joseph. Preface. *The Nigger of the "Narcissus."* Ed. Robert Kimbrough. New York: Norton. 1979. 145–48.

————. *Heart of Darkness and The Secret Sharer*. New York: Bantam, 1969.

Corrigan, Timothy. *New German Film: The Displaced Image*. Austin: U of Texas P, 1983.

Cowie, Peter. *Ingmar Bergman: A Critical Biography*. New York: Scribner's,1982.

Crabbe, Katharyn. "Lean's 'Oliver Twist': Novel to Film." *Film Criticism* 2.1 (1977): 46–51.

Culler, Jonathan. *Structuralist Poetics*. Ithaca: Cornell UP, 1975.

Currie, Gregory. *Image and Mind: Film, Philosophy, and Cognitive Science*. New York: Cambridge UP, 1995.

Dixon, Wheeler Winston. *It Looks at You: The Returned Gaze of Cinema*. Albany: State University of New York P, 1995.

Docherty, Thomas. *Reading (Absent) Character*. New York: Oxford UP, 1983.

Donner, Jorn. "The Role of Jons in *The Seventh Seal*." *The Classic Cinema*. Ed. Stanley J. Solomon. New York: Harcourt Brace Jovanovich, 1973. 238–45.

Eco, Umberto. *The Role of the Reader*. Bloomington: Indiana UP, 1979.

Ellis, John. *Visible Fictions*. Boston: Routledge & Kegan Paul, 1982.

Faulkner, William. *Light in August*. New York: Modern Library, 1968.

Festinger, Leon. *A Theory of Cognitive Dissonance*. Stanford: Stanford UP, 1957.

Fischer, Lucy. "The Lady Vanishes: Women, Magic, and the Movies." *Film Before Griffith*. Ed. John Fell. Berkeley: U of California P, 1983. 339–54.

Fitzgerald, F. Scott. *The Last Tycoon*. New York: Scribner's, 1941.

————. *The Great Gatsby*. New York: Scribner's, 1925.

Fredericksen, Don. "Modes of Reflexive Film." *Quarterly Review of Film Studies* 4.3 (1979): 299–320.

Friedberg, Anne. *Window Shopping: Cinema and the Postmodern*. Berkeley: U of California P, 1993.

Frow, John. "Spectacle Binding: On Character." *Poetics Today* 7.2 (1986): 227–49.

Gado, Frank. *The Passion of Ingmar Bergman*. Durham: Duke UP, 1986.

Gass, William H. *Fiction and the Figures of Life*. New York: Knopf, 1970.

Gunning, Tom. "Phantom Images and Modern Manifestations: Spirit Photography, Magic Theater, Trick Films, and Photography's Uncanny." *Fugitive Images: From Photography to Video*. Ed. Patrice Petro. Bloomington and Indianapolis: Indiana UP, 1995.

Hake, Sabine. "Self-Referentiality in Early German Cinema." *Cinema Journal* 31.3 (1992): 37–55.

Halliwell, Leslie. *The Dead That Walk*. New York: Continuum, 1988.

Harvey, W. J. *Character in the Novel*. Ithaca: Cornell UP, 1965.

Henderson, Brian. "Exploring *Badlands*." *Wide Angle* 5.4 (1983): 38–51.

Higashi, Sumiko. *Virgins, Vamps, and Flappers*. Montreal: Eden P, 1978.

Higgins, Lynn A. *New Novel, New Wave, New Politics*. Lincoln: U of Nebraska P, 1996.

Hochman, Baruch. *Character in Literature*. Ithaca: Cornell UP, 1985.

Holmlund, Chris. "Reading Character with a Vengeance: The *Fatal Attraction* Phenomenon." *The Velvet Light Trap* 27 (spring 1991): 25–36.

Jameson, Fredric. *Postmodernism*. Durham: Duke UP, 1991.

Kael, Pauline. "The Current Cinema." Rev. of *The Last Tycoon*. *New Yorker* 29 (November 1976): 159–60.

Kawin, Bruce. Rev. of *Nosferatu*. *Film Quarterly* 33.3 (1980): 45–47.

Landy, Marcia, and Lucy Fischer. "*Dead Again* or A-Live Again: Postmodern or Postmortem?" *Cinema Journal* 33.4 (1994): 3–21.

le Carré, John. *A Perfect Spy*. New York: Knopf, 1986.

———. *The Spy Who Came in from the Cold*. New York: Coward-McCann, 1964.

Leff, Leonard J. "Reading *Kane*." *Film Quarterly* 39.1 (Fall 1985): 10–21.

Leitch, Thomas M. "Twice-Told Tales: The Rhetoric of the Remake." *Literature/Film Quarterly* 18.3 (1990): 138–49.

Lindberg, Gary. *The Confidence Man in American Literature*. New York: Oxford UP, 1982.

Livingston, Paisley. "Characterization and Fictional Truth in the Cinema." *Post-Theory: Reconstructing Film Studies*. Ed. David Bordwell and Noel Carroll. Madison: U of Wisconsin P, 1996. 149–74.

————. *Ingmar Bergman and the Rituals of Art*. Ithaca: Cornell UP, 1982.

Macklin, Anthony. "*Five Easy Pieces*: An Enigma." *Film Heritage* 6.2 (winter 1970–71): 1–10.

Malle, Louis, and Patrick Modiano. *Lacombe, Lucien*. New York: Viking, 1975.

Martin, Troy Kennedy. *Ace of Spies*. New York: Stein and Day, 1967.

Mayne, Judith. "Herzog, Murnau, and the Vampire." *The Films of Werner Herzog*. Ed. Timothy Corrigan. New York: Methuen, 1986. 119–32.

McConnell, Frank D. *The Spoken Seen*. Baltimore: Johns Hopkins UP, 1975.

Melville, Herman. *The Confidence Man*. New York: Holt, Rinehart and Winston, 1967.

Metz, Christian. *The Imaginary Signifier*. Trans. Celia Britton et al. Bloomington: Indiana UP, 1982.

————. *Film Language: A Semiotics of the Cinema*. Trans. Michael Taylor. New York: Oxford UP, 1974.

Monaghan, David. *The Novels of John le Carré*. Oxford: Basil Blackwell, 1985.

Nichols, Bill. *Representing Reality*. Bloomington: Indiana UP, 1991.

————. "The Voice of Documentary." *Film Quarterly* 36.3 (spring 1983): 17–30.

Orr, John. *Cinema and Modernity*. Cambridge: Polity P, 1993.

Oudart, Jean-Pierre. "Cinema and Suture." *Screen* 18 (winter 1977–78): 35–47.

Paletz, Gabriel. Rev. of *Daddy Nostalgia*. *Film Quarterly* 45.3 (spring 1992): 45–49.

Panofsky, Erwin. "Style and Medium in the Motion Picture." *Film*. Ed. Daniel Talbot, New York: Simon and Schuster, 1959.

Parker, Gillian. Rev. of *The Lacemaker*. *Film Quarterly* 32.1 (fall 1978): 51–55.

P. D. Z. Rev. of *The Day of the Jackal*. *Newsweek* 28 (May 1973): 101.

Petruso, Thomas E. *Life Made Real: Characterization and the Novel since Proust and Joyce*. Ann Arbor: U of Michigan P, 1991.

Peucker, Brigitte. "In Quest of the Sublime." *New German Filmmakers.* Ed. Klaus Phillips. New York: Ungar, 1984.

Phelan, James. *Reading People, Reading Plots.* Chicago: U of Chicago P, 1989.

Pierson, John. *Spike, Mike, Slackers & Dykes.* New York: Hyperion, 1995.

Postman, Neil. *Amusing Ourselves to Death.* New York: Viking Penguin, 1985.

Prawer, S. S. *Caligari's Children: The Film as Tale of Terror.* New York: Oxford UP, 1980.

Price, Martin. *Forms of Life: Character and Moral Imagination in the Novel.* New Haven: Yale UP, 1983.

Quart, Leonard, and Barbara Quart. Rev. of *The Last Tycoon. Cineaste* (winter 1976–77): 46.

Rafferty, Terrence. "True Detective." Rev. of *The Thin Blue Line. New Yorker* 5 (September 1988): 76–77.

Ray, Robert. *A Certain Tendency of the Hollywood Cinema, 1938–88.* Princeton: Princeton UP, 1985.

Rosenberg, Brian. *Little Dorrit's Shadows: Character and Contradiction in Dickens.* Columbia: U of Missouri P, 1996.

Shaffer, Lawrence. "Night for Day, Film for Life." *Film Quarterly* 28.1 (1974): 2–8.

Siegel, Joel E. "*Five Easy Pieces*: A Fraud." *Film Heritage* 6.2 (winter 1970–71): 11–13.

Simon, John. *Ingmar Bergman Directs.* New York: Harcourt Brace Jovanovich.

Smith, Murray. *Engaging Characters: Fiction, Emotion, and the Cinema.* Oxford: Oxford UP, 1995.

———. "Altered States: Character and Emotional Response in the Cinema." *Cinema Journal* 33.4 (1994): 34–56.

Smith, Paul. "The Unknown Center of Ourselves: Schefer's Writing on the Cinema." *Enclitic* 7 (fall 1982): 32–38.

Smoles, Fredric Paul. Rev. of *The Thin Blue Line. Nation* 21 (November 1988): 542–43.

Sobchack, Vivian. *The Address of the Eye.* Princeton: Princeton UP, 1992.

Sontag, Susan. *On Photography*. New York: Farrar, Straus and Giroux, 1977.

——. "Film and Theatre." *Film Theory and Criticism*. Ed. Gerald Mast and Marshall Cohen. 1st ed. New York: Oxford UP, 1974. 249–67.

——. *Styles of Radical Will*. New York: Dell, 1969.

Staiger, Janet. *Interpreting Films*. Princeton: Princeton UP, 1992.

Stam, Robert. *Reflexivity in Film and Literature*. New York: Columbia UP, 1992.

Stam, Robert, Robert Burgoyne, and Sandy Flitterman-Lewis. *New Vocabularies in Film Semiotics*. London: Routledge, 1992.

Starr, Cecile. *Discovering the Movies*. New York: Van Nostrand Reinhold, 1972.

Steene, Birgitta. *Ingmar Bergman: A Guide to References and Resources*. Boston: G. K. Hall, 1987.

Strick, Philip. Rev. of *Nosferatu—the Vampyre*. *Sight and Sound* 48.2 (1979): 127–28.

Surmelian, Leon. *Techniques of Fiction Writing*. New York: Doubleday, 1968.

Todd, Janet. "The Classic Vampire." *The English Novel and the Movies*. Ed. Michael Klein and Gillian Parker. New York: Ungar. 197–210.

Van Wert, William. "Psychoanalysis and Con Games." *Film Quarterly* 43.4 (1990): 2–10.

Vernet, Marc. "The Look at the Camera." Trans. Dana Polan. *Cinema Journal* 28.2 (winter 1989): 48–63.

Walker, Beverly. "Malick on Badlands." *Sight and Sound* 76.2 (spring 1975): 82–83.

Warshow, Robert. *The Immediate Experience*. Garden City: Doubleday, 1962.

West, Nathanael. *The Complete Works of Nathanael West*. New York: Farrar, Straus and Giroux, 1957.

Williams, Linda. "Mirrors Without Memories: Truth, History and the New Documentary." *Film Quarterly* 46.3 (1993): 9–21.

Wilson, George. *Narration in Light: Studies in Cinematic Point of View*. Baltimore: Johns Hopkins UP, 1986.

Wilson, Rawdon. "The Bright Chimera: Character as a Literary Term." *Critical Inquiry* 5 (1979): 725–49.

Wood, Michael. *America in the Movies*. New York: Basic Books, 1975.

Zinnemann, Fred. *A Life in the Movies: An Autobiography*. New York: Scribner's, 1992.

ABOUT THE AUTHOR

———————— ◈ ————————

Lloyd Michaels is Frederick F. Seely Professor of English at Allegheny College, where he has taught courses in literature and film since 1972. For the past twenty years he has edited *Film Criticism*, the third oldest film journal in continuous publication in America. He is the author of *Elia Kazan: A Guide to References and Resources* (G. K. Hall). His articles and reviews have appeared in *Film Quarterly*, *Post-Script*, *University of Toronto Quarterly*, *New Orleans Review*, *Literature/Film Quarterly*, *Cinema nuovo*, *Western Humanities Review*, *Studies in the Humanities*, and *Film Criticism*, and he has contributed essays to *Magill's Survey of Cinema* and *The International Dictionary of Films and Filmmaking*.

INDEX

◈

Abbot and Costello Meet Frankenstein (1948), 69

absence. *See* presence of absence

acting. *See* performance style (strategy for presenting character)

Adams, Randall Dale, 103–11, 114, 117, 169n. 30, 170nn. 31–32

adaptation, 67–82, 84

Addway, Norman, 88

Aguirre, Wrath of God (1972), 76, 168n. 22

aliens, 44

Allen, Woody, 140. *See also Manhattan; Zelig*

Amants, Les (1958), 131

Andersson, Bibi, 35, 36

Andrew, Dudley, 105

Anspach, Susan, 153

Antonioni, Michelangelo, 18

apparatus, cinematic, 71; Baudry's theory, 2, 49, 68, 83; and magicians, 57, 59. *See also* film projection

Aristotle, 1

Armoire des frères Davenport, L' (1902), 6

Arnheim, Rudolf, 6, 7

art cinema, xv, 16, 25, 26, 85, 134

Au revoir les enfants (1987), 131, 171n. 44

Autumn Sonata (1978), 48

Avventura, L' (1960), 26

Badham, John, 68, 69

Badlands (1973), 142–50

Barrymore, John, 25

Barthes, Roland, xiii, 1, 2, 11, 12, 36, 37, 44, 119

Baudelaire, Charles, 129

Baudrillard, Louis, 61

Baudry, Jean-Louis, 2, 49, 83

Bazin, André, xv, 6, 7, 11, 150, 171n. 44

Beatty, Warren, 169n. 26

Beaumont, Francis: *The Knight of the Burning Pestle*, 51

Being There (1979), 25, 83

Bell, Tom, 94

Bellow, Saul, 96

Beneyton, Yves, 157

Bening, Annette, 53

Benjamin, Walter, 68

Bergman, Ingmar, 5–6, 25, 48–49, 64, 162, 167n. 14, 170n. 33. *See also The Magician; The Passion of Anna; Persona*

Bergman, Ingrid, 126

Berry, Dennis, 134

Bettelheim, Bruno, 96

Birkin, Jane, 134, 138

Bjornstrand, Gunnar, 54

Black, Karen, 152
Blaise, Pierre, 130, 133–34
Blow Up (1966), 18
Body Heat (1981), 9–10
Bogarde, Dirk, 134, 136
Bogart, Humphrey, 8, 10, 126, 169n. 28
Bogdanovich, Peter, 13
Bordwell, David, 16, 18, 28
Bram Stoker's Dracula (1992), 68, 69, 71, 75, 168n. 19
Brandauer, Klaus Maria, 140
Brando, Marlon, 10, 119–20
Braudy, Leo, 24–25, 43–44, 49
Brecht, Bertolt, 1, 2, 51
Browning, Tod, 68, 69, 75, 76
Bryant, Michael, 87–88
Buffy the Vampire Killer (1994), 69
Burton, Richard, 84, 168–69n. 24
Butch Cassidy and the Sundance Kid (1969), 52, 167n. 14

Cabaret (1972), 170n. 36
Cabinet of Dr. Caligari, The (1919), 25, 74
Carné, Marcel, 136
Carroll, Noël, 8
Casablanca (1942), 126
casting (strategy for presenting character), 9, 10, 11, 134, 165n. 3
Cavell, Stanley, xv, 2, 6–7, 129–30
Cayla, Adrien, 20
Chaplin, Charles, 128, 150, 152
Chirico, Giorgio de, 139, 140
cinema of attractions, 71, 83, 95, 101
cinéma vérité, 103, 105, 110, 169n. 29
ciphers, 24, 31, 83, 95–99
Citizen Kane (1941), 8, 16–17, 96, 101; and character representation, 9, 11, 15, 28–32, 114, 147, 152; and Welles's career, 13, 120, 142
Cixous, Hélène, xiv
Clément, Aurore, 130

cognitive dissonance, 110, 117
Cole, Nat King, 144, 146
Coleridge, Samuel Taylor, 49, 51
color as a deceptive signifier, 107
colorization, 13
Confidence Man, The (novel by Herman Melville), 48, 49–50, 53, 66
confidence men, 24, 31, 47–66, 167n. 13
Conrad, Joseph, 3, 9, 84, 127, 168n. 23
Coppola, Francis, 68, 69, 71, 75, 131, 168n. 19
Cotten, Joseph, 48
Cries and Whispers (1972), 45
Crouse, Lindsay, 60
Crowley, Jeananne, 88
Crying Game, The (1992), 31, 95
Curtis, Tony, 126
Cusack, John, 53

Daddy Nostalgia (1990), 134, 136–38
Damned, The (1969), 134
Day of the Jackal (1973), 18, 20–24, 26, 85, 101
Day of the Locust, The (1975), 122
Days of Heaven (1978), 142, 144, 147–52
Dead Poet's Society, The (1989), 10
Dean, James, 143, 144, 171–72n. 45
Death in Venice (1970), 134
deconstructionism, 102
DeNiro, Robert, 121–22
Despair (1978), 134
dialogue (strategy for presenting character), 9, 11, 62, 69,114
direct address, 105, 169n. 29
discourse, in *The Thin Blue Line*, 103–4, 105–8, 109–10, 114
Dr. Jekyll and Mr. Hyde (1932, 1941), 16, 25
documentary film, xiv, 129–30, 169n. 29; *The Thin Blue Line*, 101–17

doppelgangers. *See* doubles
doubles, 24–26, 31, 34, 44, 50,
    165n. 1; in *Badlands*, 143; in
    Citizen Kane, 28–29; in *Dr.
    Jekyll and Mr. Hyde*, 25, 68; in
    Dracula films, 67, 68, 69, 75; in
    Five Easy Pieces, 153; in *The
    Last Tycoon*, 124–25; in *The
    Magician*, 55–57; as monsters,
    67, 68, 83; in *Persona*, 34, 44; in
    The Thin Blue Line, 111
Doyle, Sir Arthur Conan, 11
Dracula (1931, Tod Browning), 68,
    69, 75, 76
Dracula (1978, John Badham), 68,
    69
Dracula (novel by Bram Stoker), 67,
    68, 69, 71
dramatic monologue, 152–56

East of Eden (1955), 171–72n. 45
Eastwood, Clint, 10, 18, 101
Eco, Umberto, xiii-xiv
Egan, Peter, 88
Eisner, Lotte, 70, 75
Ekerot, Bengt, 55, 57
elegy (narrative mode), 13–15, 31,
    125, 127, 138
Eliot, T. S., 128
Elmer Gantry (1960), 49, 167n. 13
entropy, 13–15, 119–38; in *Citizen
    Kane*, 29–30; in Dracula films,
    68–69; in *Persona*, 46; in *Reilly:
    Ace of Spies*, 92; in *The Thin
    Blue Line*, 114
Escape from Alcatraz (1979),
    17–18, 19
*Every Man for Himself and God
    Against All. See The Mystery of
    Kaspar Hauser*
existentialism, 45, 46
expressionism, 48; in Herzog's
    films, 72, 76, 97, 99; in
    Murnau's *Nosferatu*, 70, 72; in
    The Thin Blue Line, 102–3, 104,
    105–6, 110

Face in the Crowd, A (1957), 49,
    167n. 13
Face to Face (1976), 35
Fanny and Alexander (1982), 54
Farrow, Mia, 96
Faulkner, William, 9, 111
Femme Nikita, La (1990), 13
fiction, 31, 51, 103, 111; compared
    with film, 1–5, 9, 12, 13, 15, 41,
    162; novel into film, 85, 122–23
Fielding, Henry: *Joseph Andrews*,
    51
Film Criticism, xiii, 166n. 8
film noir, 53
film projection, 9, 48–49, 78, 150,
    161; and entropy, 7, 8, 13, 64,
    124, 140; in *Persona*, 36, 37, 39,
    41–43
Fisher King, The (1991), 10
Fisher, Terence, 68, 69
Fitzgerald, F. Scott, 121–27
Five Easy Pieces (1970), 152–56
Flaherty, Robert, 102
Fleming, Ian, 87, 91
Fleming, Victor, 25
formalism, xiii–xiv, 2, 43
Forrest Gump (1994), 101
Forster, E. M., xiv
Forsyth, Frederick: *The Day of the
    Jackal*, 18, 20
400 Blows, The (1959), 114
Fowles, John, 48
Fox, Edward, 18
Frears, Stephen, 51
Freud, Sigmund, 70
Friday the 13th (film cycle), 16
Friedrich, Caspar David, 75

Gable and Lombard (1976), 122
Gambler, The (1974), 16, 17
Garland, Judy, 170n. 36
Gershwin, George, 121
ghosts, 67, 147, 148, 150, 152; as
    character types, 31, 55–57, 143,
    171n. 40
Giant (1956), 144

Gide, André, 51
Gieshe, Thérèse, 130, 134
Giorgetti, Florence, 157
Glass, Philip, 106
Godard, Jean-Luc, 157
Good Morning Vietnam (1987), 10
Goretta, Claude, 157–62
Gounod, Charles, 76, 78
Grant, Cary, 35, 48
Great Balls of Fire (1989), 171n. 41
*Great Ecstasy of the Woodsculptor
    Steiner, The* (1974), 76
Great Frenzy, The (1975), 134
Great Train Robbery, The (1903), 6
Greene, Graham, 84, 168n. 23
Greene, Robert: *A Notable Discovery
    of Cozenage*, 50–51, 52, 64
Grierson, John, 102, 105
Griffith, D. W., 3, 9
Grifters, The (1990), 50, 51, 52–54,
    60, 61

Hardy Boys, The (novel series by
    Edward L. Stratemeyer), 171n. 43
Harlan County, U.S.A. (1976), 110
Harris, David, 103, 104, 106–7, 108,
    110–17
Harvest of Shame (1960), 102
Hauser, Kaspar, 96. *See also The
    Mystery of Kaspar Hauser*
Heart of Glass (1976), 75–76
Hearts of the West (1975), 122
Hemingway, Margot, 120
Hemingway, Mariel, 120, 170n. 35
Herzog, Werner, 75–76, 168n. 22,
    169n. 27. *See also The Mystery
    of Kaspar Hauser; Nosferatu, the
    Vampyre*
Hill, George Roy, 51, 52, 167n. 14
Hiroshima, Mon Amour (1959), 144
Hitchcock, Alfred, 24–25
horror films, 44, 68, 75, 84
Horror of Dracula (1958), 68, 69
Hour of the Wolf (1968), 48, 54
House of Games (1987), 31, 51–52,
    53–54, 59–66, 168n. 18

Howe, Irving, 96
humanism, xvi, 4, 35, 162
Huppert, Isabelle, 157, 161
Hurt, William, 10
Huston, Angelica, 53

identification, 7
imaginary signifier, 34–43, 48, 114;
    in *Marianne and Juliane*, 16–17;
    Metz's theory, 7, 11–12, 34–36,
    43, 68, 78, 104; in *Nosferatu, the
    Vampyre*, 78; in *Persona*, 35,
    36–43, 166n. 8; in *The Sting*, 53.
    See also presence of absence
Immigrant, The (1917), 150, 171n.
    44
In the Line of Fire (1993), 25, 101
intertextuality, 126

Jameson, Fredric, xvi, 121, 127, 162
Jewel in the Crown, The (television
    production), 86
Jones, James: *The Thin Red Line*,
    171n. 41
Jordan, Neil, 95
Joseph Andrews (novel by Henry
    Fielding), 51
Josephson, Erland, 54
Joyce, Adrien, 152
Joyce, James, 9
Jules and Jim (1961), 127–30, 131,
    133, 136; Catherine, 13–15, 26,
    120, 128–30

Kael, Pauline, 122
Kazan, Elia, 121–22, 126–27, 171n.
    38, 171–72n. 45
Keaton, Buster, 140
Kinski, Klaus, 68–69, 74, 75
Kinski, Nastassja, 166n. 5
Knight of the Burning Pestle, The
    (drama by Francis Beaumont), 51
Kracauer, Siegfried, 30

Lacan, Jacques, 11, 35, 60, 78
Lacemaker, The (1977), 157–62

Lacombe, Lucien (1974), 127–28, 130–36
Lady from Shanghai (1948), 16
Langella, Frank, 68–69
Lanzmann, Claude, 102
Last Laugh, The (1924), 72
Last Picture Show, The (1971), 13
Last Tycoon, The (1976), 13, 121–28, 171n. 38
Last Year at Marienbad (1961), 16, 26
Laure, Odette, 136
le Carré, John, 84–85, 87, 90, 91, 95, 168–69nn. 23–24
Lee, Christopher, 68–69
Lermontov, Mikhail, 41
Life and Times of Rosie the Riveter, The (1980), 110
Lithgow, John, 169n. 28
Little Drummer Girl, The (1984), 84
Lockhart, Robin Bruce, 94
Lorre, Peter, 75
lost object, 31, 131; in Dracula films, 69–70, 76, 77–78; Metz's theory, xvi, 11, 30, 35, 119
Lowenadler, Holger, 130
Lugosi, Bela, 68–69, 75
Lukacs, Georg, 71
Lumière, Auguste and Louis, 5, 16

Macbeth (1971), 74
Magician, The (1958), 45, 51–52, 53–59, 60, 64; Spegel, 142, 143, 167–68n. 16; Vogler, 25, 37, 64
Magnificent Ambersons, The (1942), 142
Magritte, René, 51
Malick, Terrence, 142, 144, 146, 147, 150, 171nn. 41, 43
Malle, Louis, 128, 130–31, 133, 136, 140, 171nn. 39, 44
Mamet, David, 51–52, 59–66
Mamoulian, Rouben, 25,
Manhattan (1979), 120–21, 170n. 35

Mann, Thomas, 48
Mantegna, Joe, 60
Manz, Linda, 147, 148
March, Fredric, 25
March of Time series, 105
Marianne and Juliane (1982), 16–17
Martin, Troy Kennedy, 86–87, 94
Mask, The (1994), 101
masks, 15–16, 17–18, 44–45, 55, 58, 166n. 6
Massey, Raymond, 171n. 45
Masterpiece Theatre (television series), 85, 169n. 25
McKern, Leo, 88
Mean Streets (1973), 123
Medavoy, Michael, 171n. 41
Méliès, Georges, 5, 6, 9, 16, 48, 101; phantom hearse, 72, 76–77
Melville, Herman, 12, 31; *The Confidence Man*, 48, 49–50, 53, 66
memory, 119–38, 144, 146, 147
Mephisto (1981), 140–42
Metz, Christian, 3, 12, 33, 48, 104; imaginary signifier, 7, 11–12, 34–36, 43, 68, 78, 104; lost object, xvi, 11, 30, 35, 119; presence of absence, xv, 8, 104; primordial *elsewhere*, 50, 61, 74, 97
mimesis. *See* representation
Minnelli, Liza, 170n. 36
mirrors, 15–17, 44, 77, 78, 120, 166n. 5
mise-en-scène (strategy for presenting character), 9, 11, 36, 77, 85
Miss Lonelyhearts (novel by Nathanael West), 64
modernism, xv, 51–52, 71, 83
Modiano, Patrick, 133, 171n. 39
monologue, dramatic, 152–53, 156
Monroe, Marilyn, 157
monsters, 31, 44, 67, 68, 83
Moore, Demi, 13
Moore, Roger, 88

Moreau, Jeanne, 13–14, 16, 126, 128
Morris, Errol. *See The Thin Blue Line*
Murder One (television program), 86
Murnau, F. W. *See Nosferatu, a Symphony of Horror*
musical score, 58–59, 102, 106, 121, 131, 133, 147, 153; in *Nosferatu, the Vampyre*, 74, 75, 76, 78; specific song titles, 126, 138, 144, 146
Mystery (television series), 169n. 25
Mystery of Kaspar Hauser, The (1974), 75–76, 96–99, 169n. 27

Nabokov, Vladimir, 48
narrative, xiv, 2, 85, 138; film as, 4, 26, 127; modes, 31; narrational devices, xvi-xvii, 41; structure, 62, 69
Neill, Sam, 88
New Criticism, xiii, 1, 2
New German Cinema, 72
New Wave, 13, 128, 129, 131
Newman, Paul, 52
newsreel footage, 8, 101, 102, 129–30
Nicholson, Jack, 152
Night Mail (1936), 102
Night Porter, The (1974), 134
Nighy, Bill, 89
nonfiction film. *See* documentary film
Nosferatu, a Symphony of Horror (1922), 67–76, 78–79, 83, 167–68n. 16, 168n. 20
Nosferatu, the Vampyre (1979), 67–82, 83, 167–68n. 16, 168nn. 21–22, 172n. 45
nostalgia, 8, 13, 119–38
Nouvelle Vague. *See* New Wave
novel. *See* fiction

Oldham, Gary, 68–69
Olivier, Laurence, 8

On the Waterfront (1954), 10, 119–20, 127
Ophuls, Marcel, 131

Paris, Texas (1984), 16, 166n. 5
Passion of Anna, The (1969), 45, 166–67n. 10
Pawlo, Tovio, 54
Pearce, Joanne, 94
Perfect Spy, A (television film, 1987), 84, 85
performance style (strategy for presenting character), 9, 10, 62, 69, 134
Persona (1966), 16, 26, 33–46, 47, 114, 116–67nn. 8–11, 170n. 37; artist in, 25, 48, 54, 67–68
photography, xiv, 2, 3, 5, 6, 167n. 11
Pinter, Harold, 121–22
Plato, 1, 51
Pleasence, Donald, 123
plot. *See* narrative
Polanski, Roman, 74, 114
Popul Vuh, 74, 75
pornography (narrative mode), 31
Porter, Edwin S., 6–7
postmodernism, xv, 83, 140; in *House of Games*, 52, 61, 62, 64; Jameson's description, xvi, 127, 162; in *The Thin Blue Line*, 102, 103, 114
poststructuralism, xiii, 2
presence of absence, xv, 5–9, 16, 31, 101, 165n. 3; in *Badlands*, 146; in *The Cabinet of Dr. Caligari*, 25; in *Citizen Kane*, 8, 28, 30; in *Daddy Nostalgia*, 136; in *The Day of the Jackal*, 22–24, 166n. 7; in Dracula films, 72, 76; in *Five Easy Pieces*, 152–53; in *House of Games*, 64; in Jules and Jim, 128; in *Lacombe, Lucien*, 133–34, in *The Last Tycoon*, 125–26; in *The Magician*, 55, 57; in *Persona*, 34,

36, 41, 43; in *Reilly: Ace of Spies*, 86, 95; in *The Sting*, 53; in *The Thin Blue Line*, 108, 111, 114
Prévert, Jacques, 136
Price, Vincent, 87–88
Prison (1949), 44
Propp, Vladimir, 2, 74
Protheride, Brian, 91
Proust, Marcel, 9
Providence (1977), 136
psychological interpretation of character, 35, 66, 87–88, 146–47, 162; in *Citizen Kane*, 30; in Dracula films, 70, 74; in *The Grifters*, 53
Purple Rose of Cairo, The (1985), 140

Rafelson, Bob, 152, 156
Raging Bull (1980), 17
Rashomon (1950), 26
Redford, Robert, 52
Reds (1981), 169n. 26
reflexivity, 31, 53, 60, 95, 96, 128, 150, 166n. 6; in *Badlands*, 143, 146; in Dracula films, 68, 70, 71, 72, 77–78, 168n. 19; in *The Last Tycoon*, 122, 125; in *The Magician*, 58, 168n. 17; in *Persona*, 33–46; in *The Thin Blue Line*, 102, 104, 105, 114. *See also* confidence men; doubles; masks; mirrors; spies
Reilly: Ace of Spies (television film series, 1984), 31, 85–95
Reisz, Karel, 17
Renoir, Jean, 136
representation, xiv, 1–32, 58, 71, 103, 171n. 40
Repulsion (1965), 111, 114
Reservoir Dogs (1992), 26–28
Resnais, Alain, 68, 136, 157
Reversal of Fortune (1993), 1, 31–32
Ricoeur, Paul, 105
Ritt, Martin, 84, 168–69n. 24

Riva, Emmanuele, 144
Roger and Me (1989), 110–11
Rohmer, Eric, 157
Rose, Gus, 109, 111, 169n. 30
Rossellini, Isabella, 169n. 28
Russia House, The (1990), 84

S., Bruno, 97, 169n. 17
Saint, Eva Marie, 10
Sawdust and Tinsel (1953), 54
Schmidt-Reitwein, Jorg, 75
Schreck, Max, 68–69, 74, 75
Scorsese, Martin, 17
Sellers, Peter, 25, 97
semiotics. *See* structuralism
Seventh Seal, The (1957), 45, 54, 57, 59
sex, lies, and videotape (1989), 140
Shadow of a Doubt (1943), 24–25, 48
shadows, 97–99, 111, 139, 166n. 5; in Dracula films, 71, 72, 77, 78, 167–68n. 16
Shakespeare, 74, 87, 94–95, 165n. 4
Shame (1968), 48, 54
Sheen, Martin, 142
Shelley, Mary, 67
Shepard, Sam, 148
Sherlock, Jr. (1924), 140
Shoah (1985), 102
Siegel, Don, 166n. 6
Smiley's People (television film, 1982), 84
Soderbergh, Steven, 140
Sontag, Susan, 12, 15, 33–34, 41, 43, 96, 166n. 8, 167n. 11
Sophie's Choice (1982), 10
Sorrow and the Pity, The (1971), 131
sound track. *See* musical score
Spacek, Sissy, 142, 148
special effects, 6, 72, 75–76, 77, 102, 105–6
spectres. *See* ghosts
Spiegel, Sam, 121
Spielberg, Steven, 13

spies, 24, 31, 83–95, 97, 168n. 23
Spirit of the Beehive, The (1973), 76
spirit photography, 165n. 1
spirits. *See* ghosts
Spy Who Came in from the Cold, The (1965), 84
Stanton, Harry Dean, 166n. 5
Star 80 (1983), 120
star system. *See* casting
stereotypes. *See* typology
Sterne, Laurence: *Tristram Shandy,* 51
Stevens, George, 144
Stevenson, Robert Louis, 67
Sting, The (1973), 31, 50, 51, 52–54, 60, 61
Stoker, Bram: *Dracula,* 67, 68, 69, 71
Stratemeyer, Edward L.: *The Hardy Boys,* 171n. 43
Streep, Meryl, 10
Strindberg, August, 129
Stroszek (1977), 169n. 27
structuralism, xiii, xiv, xv, xvi, 2, 35, 49
Suspicion (1941), 48
Swiss Family Robinson (novel by J. R. Wyss), 171n. 43
Sydow, Max von, 54
Szabo, Istvan, 140, 142

Taking of Pelham One Two Three, The (1974), 17
Tales from the Crypt (television series), 169n. 28
Talk Radio (1988), 167n. 13
Tanner, Alain, 157
Tarantino, Quentin, 26
Tavernier, Bertrand, 128, 134, 136, 138, 140
Taxi Driver (1976), 17
television, 84, 85–86, 162, 165n. 2
Thalberg, Irving, 121
theater, 7, 31, 51, 161; compared with film, 8, 12, 13, 15, 61, 162

Thin Blue Line, The (1987), 101–17, 142, 169n. 30, 170nn. 31–32, 34
Through a Glass Darkly (1962), 37
Thulin, Ingrid, 55
Times of Harvey Milk, The (1984), 102
Tinker, Tailor, Soldier, Spy (television film, 1980), 84, 85
Tolstoy, Leo, 3–4, 5, 124, 162
Tootsie (1982), 31
Topor, Roland, 75
Toto the Hero (1992), 140
Touch, The (1971), 45
Tracy, Spencer, 25
Tristram Shandy (novel by Laurence Sterne), 51
Triumph of the Will (1935), 11
Trotta, Margarethe von, 16–17
Truffaut, François, xvi, 114, 140; *Jules and Jim,* 13–15, 128–30, 131, 133, 136
Turner, Kathleen, 10
Twain, Mark, 48, 171n. 43
typology (strategy for presenting character), 2, 5, 9, 10, 11, 47, 140; challenged in specific films, 26, 86–89, 104

Ullmann, Liv, 35, 36

vampires, 34, 44, 67–82, 83, 160
Van Dormael, Jaco, 140
Vanishing Lady, The (1896), 5
vérité. *See* cinéma vérité
Vermeer, Jan, 161–62
Vigo, Jean, 136
voiceover: in *Badlands* and *Days of Heaven,* 142–52; in *Daddy Nostalgia,* 136; in documentaries, 87, 102, 108; in *The Last Tycoon,* 124–25; in *Persona,* 39; in *Reilly: Ace of Spies,* 92; in *The Thin Blue Line,* 105, 109

W. C. Fields and Me (1976), 122
Wagner, Richard, 75

Welles, Orson: *Citizen Kane*, 9, 13, 15, 28, 30, 31, 142, 147, 152
Wenders, Wim, 166n. 5, 168n. 21
West, Nathanael, 48, 50, 64
Williams, Robin, 10
Wings of Desire (1988), 168n. 21
"wrong man" theme, 103–5, 108
Wynette, Tammy, 153

Wyss, J. R.: *The Swiss Family Robinson*, 171n. 43

Zapruder, Abraham, 166n. 7
Zazie dans le métro (1960), 131
Zelig (1983), 25, 95–97, 101, 102, 169n. 26
Zinnemann, Fred, 20–24, 85

DATE DUE

MAY 0 9 1998			